THE
UNIVERSAL HUMAN

THE
UNIVERSAL HUMAN
The Evolution of Individuality

Four Lectures given between
1909 and 1916
in Munich and Bern

Rudolf Steiner

Translation edited by
Christopher Bamford and
Sabine H. Seiler

ANTHROPOSOPHIC PRESS

The lectures in this book were published from stenographic records not revised by the lecturer. "Individuality and the Group-Soul" and "The God Within and the God of Outer Revelation" appear in German in *Die tieferen Geheimnisse des Menschheitswerdens im Lichte der Evangelien* (Vol. 117 in the Collected Works). "The Lord of the Soul" is published in German in *Exkurse in das Gebiet des Markus-Evangeliums* (Vol. 124 in the Collected Works), and the German text of "The Universal Human: The Unification of Humanity through the Christ Impulse" appears in *Die geistige Vereinigung der Menschheit durch den Christus-Impuls* (Vol. 165 in the Collected Works). All three titles are published by Rudolf Steiner Verlag in Dornach, Switzerland.

All Bible quotations in this volume are taken from *The New Oxford Annotated Bible*, Standard Revised Version.

The publishers acknowledge with gratitude the help of Gilbert Church, Ph.D. who revised an earlier translation of these lectures.

Copyright ©1990
Anthroposophic Press, Inc.

Library of Congress Cataloging-in-Publication Data

Steiner, Rudolf, 1861–1925
    [Lectures. English. Selections]
    The universal human: the evolution of individuality: four lectures given between 1909 and 1916 in Munich and Bern / Rudolf Steiner; translation edited by Christopher Bamford and Sabine H. Seiler.
    Contents: Individuality and the group-soul — The God within and the God of outer revelation — The Lord of the soul — The universal human.
    ISBN 0-88010-350-7 — ISBN 0-88010-289-6 (pbk.)
    1. Anthroposophy.   I. Bamford, Christopher.   II. Seiler, Sabine H.   III. Title.

BP595.S894L4213   1990
299'.935—dc20   90-49532
                                                                 CIP

Book Design and Production by Studio 31

Contents

LECTURE ONE

Individuality and the Group-Soul

MUNICH, DECEMBER 4, 1909

TODAY WE WILL consider a general theme: the question of
the meaning and tasks of anthroposophical spiritual science.
Tomorrow we will take up a more specific theme: the
destiny and nature of the individual human being. We have
often emphasized that anthroposophy has a special task and
meaning for human beings in the present age. People who
think will not be able to avoid the question what the aims
of this spiritual movement are and how they relate to other
tasks of our time. Such tasks may be explained from diverse
points of view, as we have often done. Today we will try to
describe the evolutionary stage of contemporary humanity
and attempt to look a little into the future. Then we will
consider the task of anthroposophy in reference to our
present evolutionary stage.

We know that since the great Atlantean catastrophe,
which entirely transformed the earth, there have been five
great epochs of civilization. We designate these as the
ancient Indian, the ancient Persian, the Egypto-Chaldean,
the Greco-Latin, and the epoch we presently live in. The
latter was prepared in the eighth, ninth, and tenth centuries
after Christ; we are now actually in the middle of this
epoch. Of course, such divisions are not to be understood
as indicating that each evolutionary epoch abruptly came to
an end and then a new one began. Rather, one epoch
gradually and slowly merged into another. Long before one

7

epoch has run its course, the next one is already being prepared.

In our own cultural epoch, the fifth post-Atlantean epoch, the characteristics of the sixth epoch are already being prepared. Roughly speaking, people in our time can be divided into two groups: those who live blindly for the day, have no idea of, and know nothing about the preparation of the sixth epoch, and those who understand that something new is being prepared. The latter also know that this preparation must basically be accomplished by human beings. We find our place in our time either by passively following the customs of our society and doing what our parents have taught us to do, or by being aware that to be a conscious link in the chain of humanity we must work on ourselves and our environment to contribute, as best we can, to the preparation of what must come, namely, the sixth cultural period.

How it is possible to prepare for the sixth epoch can only be understood when we consider the character of our own period. The best way to do this is to compare it with others. We know these cultural epochs are different from each other, and over the years we have presented their various distinguishing characteristics. We have shown that in the ancient Indian period people had different soul qualities than they did later. At that time, human beings were still endowed with a high degree of clairvoyant consciousness. In later epochs, this clairvoyance was gradually lost, and perception and understanding became limited to the physical world. We have seen that the fourth epoch was slowly prepared; it was in that period that humanity came to live entirely in the physical world. This made it possible for the being whom we call Christ Jesus to incarnate in human form, as a human being on the physical plane. Next we have seen that since that time a certain stream further strengthened human capacities in the physical world. Indeed, the materialistic tendency of our age and the insistence to accept only the physical world as real are connected with humanity's further descent into the physical. However, things must not remain like this. We must ascend again into the spiritual world, bearing with us the attainments and fruits we have acquired in the physical world. It is the task of anthroposophy to offer people the possibility of ascending once again into the spiritual world.

Immediately after the great Atlantean catastrophe, there were many human beings who knew through direct perception that they were surrounded by, and lived in, a spiritual world. Gradually, however, the number of those who knew this decreased as human perception became more limited to the physical senses. In our time, the capacity to perceive the spiritual world has almost disappeared; yet something so significant is being prepared in our time that a great many people will have quite different faculties in their next incarnation. Human faculties have changed during the past five cultural epochs, and they will change again in the sixth. The capacities of a great number of people living today will change considerably in their next incarnation, as will be clear from the whole nature of their soul. Today we will talk about how different many of these human souls will be already in their next incarnation; of course, for other people, this change will not happen until two incarnations from now.

Looking at past epochs of human evolution, we can also see that the closer we come to the ancient clairvoyance, the more the human soul has the character of what we can

call "group-soulness." I have often pointed out that consciousness of this group-soulness existed preeminently among
the ancient Hebrews. A person who consciously felt himself
to be a member of this people understood, "As an individual human being, I am a transitory phenomenon, but there
lives in me something that has an immediate connection
with all the soul essence that has streamed down since the
days of our progenitor, Abraham." In esoteric terms, we
can describe these feelings of the Hebrew people as a
spiritual phenomenon. We will better understand what
happened there if we look at the following.

Let us consider a Hebrew initiate of that time. Although initiation was not so frequent among the ancient
Hebrews as among other peoples, we can characterize such
a real initiate — that is, one initiated not just into theories
and the law, but one who really saw into the spiritual
worlds — only by taking into consideration the peculiarity
of the Hebrew people as a whole. Nowadays, historians,
who are concerned only with documents, check the Old
Testament against all kinds of external records and find it
unsubstantiated. We will have occasion to point out that
the Old Testament gives us facts more faithfully than
external historical records. In any case, spiritual science
shows that the blood relationship of the Hebrews to
Abraham can really be proven, and that their claim on
Abraham as their original progenitor is fully justified. It was
known particularly in the ancient Hebrew Mystery schools
that the individuality or psychic essence of Abraham did
not incarnate only in him, but is an eternal being existing in
the spiritual world.

In fact, all true initiates among the Hebrews were
inspired by the same spirit that inspired Abraham; they

could call upon that spirit and were permeated by the same soul nature as Abraham. There was a real connection between every initiate and the tribal ancestor Abraham. This connection was expressed also in the feelings of the individuals belonging to the Hebrew people. They felt that what came to expression in Abraham was the group-soul of the people.

Group-souls were also experienced in the same way by other peoples of that time. Humanity in general goes back to group-souls. The farther back we go in human evolution, the less developed we find the individuality. Instead, a whole group belonged together as a unit, as is the case in the animal kingdom. This "groupness" is more and more pronounced the farther back we go into ancient times. Groups of human beings then belonged together, and the group-soul was considerably stronger than the individual soul.

Even today human group-soulness is still not overcome. Those who claim the opposite merely fail to take into account certain subtler phenomena of life, such as the resemblance of certain people not only in their physiognomies but also in their soul qualities. In a sense, people can be divided into categories, and everyone will fit into one of them. Individuals may differ as to this or that quality but a certain group-soulness still makes itself felt and not only because there are still different peoples. The boundaries between the nations continue to disintegrate, but other groupings are still perceptible. Thus certain basic characteristics are combined in individuals in such a way that the last vestiges of group-soulness can still be perceived today.

We are now living in a period of transition. All group-soulness must gradually be stripped off. Just as the

differences between nations are gradually disappearing, and
the factions within them come to understand each other
better, so also will other group-soul qualities have to be
shed. Instead, the individual nature of each person will be
pushed to the fore. We have here characterized something
essential in evolution. From another point of view, we can
also say that in the course of evolution the concept of race,
by which group-soulness is chiefly expressed, gradually
loses its significance.

If we go back beyond the Atlantean catastrophe, we see
how human races were prepared. In the ancient Atlantean
age, human beings were grouped according to external
bodily characteristics even more so than in our time. The
races we distinguish today are merely vestiges of these
significant differences between human beings in ancient
Atlantis. The concept of race is only fully applicable to
Atlantis. Because we are dealing with the real evolution of
humanity, we have therefore never used this concept of race
in its original meaning. Thus, we do not speak of an Indian
race, a Persian race, and so on, because it is no longer true
or proper to do so. Instead, we speak of an Indian, a
Persian, and other periods of civilization. And it would
make no sense at all to say that in our time a sixth "race" is
being prepared. Though remnants of ancient Atlantean
differences, of ancient Atlantean group-soulness, still exist
and the division into races is still in effect, what is being
prepared for the sixth epoch is precisely the stripping away
of race. That is essentially what is happening.

Therefore, in its fundamental nature, the anthroposophical movement, which is to prepare the sixth period,
must cast aside the division into races. It must seek to unite

people of all races and nations, and to bridge the divisions and differences between various groups of people. The old point of view of race has a physical character, but what will prevail in the future will have a more spiritual character.

That is why it is absolutely essential to understand that our anthroposophical movement is a spiritual one. It looks to the spirit and overcomes the effects of physical differences through the force of being a spiritual movement. Of course, any movement has its childhood illnesses, so to speak. Consequently, in the beginning of the theosophical movement the earth was divided into seven periods of time, one for each of the seven root races, and each of these root races was divided into seven sub-races. These seven periods were said to repeat in a cycle so that one could always speak of seven races and seven sub-races. However, we must get beyond the illnesses of childhood and understand clearly that the concept of race has ceased to have any meaning in our time.

Humanity is becoming evermore individual, and this has further implications for human individuality. It is important that this individuality develop in the right way. The anthroposophical movement is to help people become individualities, or personalities, in the right sense. How can it accomplish this? Here we must look to the most striking new quality of the human soul that is being prepared. People often ask why we do not remember our former incarnations. I have often answered this question, which is like saying that because a four-year-old child cannot do arithmetic, human beings cannot do arithmetic. When the child reaches ten, he or she will be able to multiply with ease. It is the same with the soul. If it cannot remember our

former incarnations today, the time will come when it will
be able to do so. Then it will possess the same capacity
initiates have.

This new development is happening today. There are
numerous souls nowadays who are so far advanced that
they are close to the moment of remembering their former
incarnations, or at least the last one. A number of people are
at the threshold of comprehensive memory, embracing life
between birth and death as well as previous incarnations.
Many people will remember their present incarnation when
they are reborn in their next life. It is simply a question of
how they remember. The anthroposophical movement is to
help and guide people to remember in the right way.

In light of this, we can describe this anthroposophical
movement as leading a person to grasp correctly what is
called the I, the innermost member of the human being. I
have often pointed out that Fichte rightly said most people
would sooner regard themselves as a piece of lava on the
moon than as an I.[1] To think how many people in our time
have any idea at all of the I — that is, of what they are
—leads to a dismal conclusion.

In this connection I am always reminded of a friend I
had more than thirty years ago and who, as a young
student, was completely steeped in the materialistic outlook. Today it is more modern to call it the "monistic"
outlook. He always laughed when he heard someone say
that within each human being there was something that
could be called a spiritual being. My friend thought that
what lives as thought in us is produced by mechanical or
chemical processes in the brain. I often said to him, "Look,
if you seriously believe this, why are you lying all the time?"
For, in fact, he really was lying continually because he never

said, "My brain feels, my brain thinks," but, "*I* think, *I* feel, *I* know this or that." Thus, he contradicted his own theory with his every word — as everyone does, for it is impossible to adhere fully to a materialistic theory one has imagined. It is impossible to remain truthful if one thinks materialistically. If one wanted to say, "My brain loves you," then one should not say "you," but "My brain loves your brain." People are not aware of the consequences of their theories. This may be humorous, but it also shows the deep foundation of unconscious untruthfulness that underlies our present spiritual condition.

Now, most people really would sooner regard themselves as a piece of lava on the moon, that is as a piece of matter, than as an I. The I can be understood least of all through science with its materialistic methods and way of thinking. How can we understand the I? How can we arrive at an idea or concept of what we feel instinctively when we say, "I think"? We can do so only through knowing on the basis of the anthroposophical world view how the human being is constituted and structured — that the physical body is related to Saturn, the etheric body to the sun, the astral body to the moon, and the I to the earth. When we keep in mind the ideas we can gather from the cosmos, we understand that the I, as the real master, works on the other members. Then we gradually come to understand what we mean by the word "I."

As we learn to understand this word, we slowly approach the highest concept of this I. We begin to feel ourselves as spiritual beings not only when we feel ourselves to be within an I, but also when we can say that something lives in our individuality that was already there before Abraham. Then we can say not only, "I and father Abraham are one," but also "I and the Father, that is, the spiritual element weaving through and living in the world, are one." What lives in the I is the same spiritual substance that lives and weaves in the world as spirit. Thus we gradually come to understand the I, the bearer of human individuality that goes from incarnation to incarnation.

How do we understand the I and the world in general through the anthroposophical world view? The anthroposophical view of the world develops in the most individual way, but at the same time it is the most unindividual thing you can imagine. It arises in the most individual way when the secrets of the cosmos are revealed in a human soul, when the great spiritual beings of the world stream into this soul. The content of the world must be experienced in the human individuality in the most individual way, but at the same time it must also be experienced completely impersonally. Concerning the true character of cosmic mysteries, we have to say that as long as we still value our personal opinion, we cannot arrive at the truth.

Indeed, it is the peculiar nature of anthroposophical truth that the observer must not hold any opinion of his or her own about it and must not have any preference for this or that theory. The observer must not like this or that view more than any other because of his or her individual peculiarities. As long as we have our own opinions, it is impossible for the true secrets of the world to be revealed to us. We must pursue knowledge quite individually, but our individuality must be so developed that it no longer retains anything personal; it must be free of sympathies and antipathies. This must be taken very seriously. Those who still prefer personal ideas and views and are inclined to this or that because of their education and temperament will never know objective truth.

This summer, we have tried to understand eastern wisdom from the standpoint of western teaching.[2] We have tried to do justice to eastern wisdom and to present it truly. It must be emphasized that if we have independent spiritual knowledge in our time, it is impossible to decide for either the oriental or the occidental views of the world on the basis of personal preference. Those who say that because of their temperament they prefer the oriental or the occidental world view and its laws do not understand what is essential here. We should not decide that Christ, let us say, is more significant than what is to be found in eastern teaching because we happen to incline toward him through our western education or temperament. We cannot answer the question how Christ is related to the orient until, from a personal standpoint, we can accept Christian and oriental teachings equally. As long as we have a preference, we are unable to make a decision. We begin to be objective only when we let the facts speak for themselves and disregard our personal opinions.

The anthroposophical world view in its true form is closely interwoven with human individuality, for this world view must spring from the I-force of the individuality and yet be independent of it. The individuality as such does not matter. The person in whom anthroposophical wisdom appears must be completely unimportant compared to this wisdom; the person as such does not matter at all. It is only essential that this person has developed so far that his or her personal likes, dislikes, and opinions do not taint the anthroposophical wisdom. Then this wisdom will indeed be individual, because the spiritual cannot appear in the light of the moon or the stars but only in the individuality, in the human soul. This individuality, however, must be developed to the point of being able to disengage from the development of the wisdom of the world.

What is entering humanity through the anthroposophical movement concerns every human being regardless of race or nationality. This movement speaks only to the new humanity, the new human being — not to an abstract concept "human being," but to every individual. This is the essential point. Anthroposophy proceeds from the individuality, the innermost core of the human being, and it speaks to and touches this core of a person's being. We usually speak to each other only as one surface to another and mostly about things not connected to our innermost being. Full understanding between individuals is hardly possible today, except when what is to be communicated comes from the center of one individual's being and speaks to and is understood rightly by the center of another. Thus, in a certain way, anthroposophy speaks a new language. Even if we are still obliged to speak in the various national languages, the content of what is said forms a new language.

What is said in the outer world is really only valid for a very limited sphere. In the past, when people still looked into the spiritual world through ancient, dreamy clairvoyance, words indicated something that existed in the spiritual world. Even in ancient Greece such things were different from what they are today. The word "idea" as used by Plato signified something different from "idea" as used by our modern philosophers, who no longer understand Plato. They have no perception of what he called "Idea," mistaking it for an abstract concept. Plato still meant something spiritual that he could perceive. Even if already rarefied, it was nevertheless something quite real. Words still contained, if I may say so, the juice of the spiritual.

The spiritual can still be traced in words. When people today use the word "wind" or "air," they mean something external, physical. However, the ancient Hebrew word for this, "Ruach," did not only refer to something physical but also to something spiritual permeating the universe. Modern materialistic science tells us that when we inhale, we simply breathe in physical air. In ancient times, however, people did not believe they inhaled only physical air; they were aware that they inhaled something spiritual, or at least something psychic.

In fact, in ancient times, words designated something spiritual and psychic. That is no longer true today; language has become limited to the external world — at least people who want to be fully up to date culturally are busy finding materialistic meanings behind terms that are obviously derived from the realm of soul and spirit. Physicists, for example, speak of an "impact" of bodies. They have forgotten that "impact" is derived from what a living being performs in its inner nature when it pushes another being. The original meaning of words is forgotten in these simple things. Thus, our language, particularly our scientific language, can no longer express anything but the material. What is in our soul while we speak can therefore be understood only by those soul faculties that are bound to the physical brain as their instrument. As a result, when the soul is disembodied, it understands nothing of all that has been said with these words. When the soul has gone through the gate of death and can no longer use the brain, all scientific discussions are quite incomprehensible to it. It does not hear or perceive what one expresses in contemporary language, which has no meaning for a disembodied soul. Our language has meaning only in the physical world.

We must consider this in relation to our way of thinking and outlook on the world because this fact is much more important than a theory. After all, what matters is life, not theory. Characteristically, one can see in the theosophical movement how materialism has crept in. Materialism sneaked even into theosophy and prevails even there, for example, in the descriptions of the etheric or life body. Rather than making an effort to understand the spiritual, people often describe the etheric body as if it were a kind of finer matter, and they do the same with the astral body. They usually begin with the physical body, proceed to the etheric or life body and say it is constructed on the same pattern as the physical body, only finer. And they continue this way until they reach nirvana. Such descriptions take their images only from the physical world.

I have even heard people say that there are fine vibrations in a room when they wanted to describe the good feeling present in the room. They do not notice that they are reducing something spiritual to matter when they think of a room as filled with vibrations as with a thin fog.

This is the most materialistic thinking possible. Materialism has taken hold even of those who want to think spiritually. This is typical of our times, and it is important that we are conscious of it. We must be especially aware that language is always a kind of tyrant over our thinking and has implanted in our souls a tendency to materialism. Many people today who claim to be idealists express themselves in an entirely materialistic way because they have been seduced, as it were, by the tyranny of language.

This materialistic language cannot be understood by the soul when it is no longer bound to the brain.

There is yet more to it than this. The method of presentation often employed in scientific-theosophical writings causes real pain to those who know occult contemplation, true spiritual perception. For this way of presentation does not make sense to people who have begun to think not with their brain but with their soul, now freed from the brain — people who really live in the spiritual world. It is all well and good to describe the world materialistically as long as we still think with the physical brain, but as soon as we begin to develop spiritual perception, speaking in this way ceases to have any meaning. Indeed, then it even causes pain to hear people say that "there are good vibrations in this room," rather than "a good feeling prevails." Because thoughts are realities, such utterances cause pain in those who can really see things spiritually. For them the room becomes filled with a dark fog when somebody expresses the thought "there are good vibrations in this room."

It is the task of our anthroposophical way of thinking, which is decidedly more important than all theories, to learn to speak a language that is understood by the soul not only while it is still in a physical body but also when it is no longer bound to the physical brain. In other words, this language must be understood by a soul still in the body and able to perceive spiritually as well as by a soul that has gone through the gate of death. That is what is important. When we use anthroposophical concepts that explain the world and the human being, we are speaking a language that can be understood here in the physical world and also by those who are no longer incarnated in physical bodies but are living between death and a new birth. Yes, what is spoken in anthroposophy is heard and understood by the so-called dead. They are fully at one with us when we speak the same language. With this language we speak to all human beings. After all, in a sense, it is mere chance whether a soul is in a body or in the condition between death and a new birth. Through anthroposophy we learn a language that is comprehensible to all human beings, living or dead. Thus, in anthroposophy we speak a language that is also spoken for the dead.

We really touch the innermost core of a person through what we cultivate in anthroposophical discussions, even if what we say appears to be abstract. We penetrate right into the human soul, and because of that, we can free people from group-soulness. Because we penetrate into their souls, they become increasingly able to really understand themselves as an I.

Interestingly, the difference between those who come to anthroposophy and really embrace it and those who do not is that the I of the former is as if crystallized into a spiritual being through anthroposophical thinking, a spiritual being that is then carried along through the gate of death. The others, who do not practice anthroposophical thinking, have a hollow space, a nothingness in the place where the I is now in physical life and after death. Any other concepts we can take in nowadays will gradually become more and more immaterial for the true core of the human soul. The central essence of the human being will be touched and understood only by the anthroposophical thoughts we take in. These crystallize a spiritual substance in us that we can take with us after death and that enables us to perceive in the spiritual world, to see and hear, and to penetrate the darkness that would otherwise exist there for us. Thus, it becomes possible that we can take the I we have developed through the anthroposophical outlook and concepts — the I that is connected to all the wisdom in the world we can receive —with us into the next incarnation. Then we will be reborn in the next incarnation with this developed I, and we will be able to remember it.

It is the deeper task of the anthroposophical movement to enable a number of human beings to enter their next incarnation with an I each remembers as his or her own, individual I. These people will then form the nucleus of the next period of civilization. Then these individuals who have been well prepared through the anthroposophical spiritual movement to remember their individual I will be spread over the earth. For the essential characteristic of the next period of civilization is that it will not be limited to particular localities, but will be spread over the whole earth. These individuals will be scattered over the earth, and thus everywhere on earth there will be a core group of people who will be crucial for the sixth epoch of civilization. These people will recognize each other as those who in their previous incarnation strove together to develop the individual I. That is the proper cultivation of that soul faculty we have spoken of.

This soul faculty will be so developed that more and more people who have not developed their I will also be able to remember their former incarnations. However, they will not remember an individual I, but only the group-I in which they had remained. In summary, people who are working in this incarnation to develop their individual I will be able to remember themselves as this or that independent individuality; they will be able to look back at the individuality they were. People who have not developed their individuality will be unable to remember any individuality.

Do not think that mere visionary clairvoyance will enable you to remember your previous I. Humanity was once clairvoyant, and if that in itself sufficed, then everyone would have remembered because all were clairvoyant. Thus, what matters is not clairvoyance; people will indeed be clairvoyant in the future. Rather, what matters is whether we have cultivated our I in this incarnation or not. If we have not cultivated it, the I will not be there as the innermost human essence, and we will remember only a group-I, only what we had in common with others. In that case we will have to look back and admit that we did not free ourselves from the group-I in this incarnation. People to whom this happens will experience it as though it were a new Fall, a second Fall of humanity, a falling back into a conscious connection with the group-soul. Not to remember oneself as an individuality and to be hemmed in by one's inability to transcend group-soulness will be something terrible in the sixth epoch. To put it bluntly, we can say that the earth and all it can yield will belong to those who now cultivate their individualities. Those, however, who do not develop their individual I will be dependent on joining a group that will instruct them in what they should think, feel, will, and do. In the future development of humanity this will be felt as a regression, a second Fall. Therefore, we should not regard the anthroposophical movement and spiritual life as mere theory but rather as something that is given to us now to prepare what is necessary for the future of humanity.

When we understand our present condition correctly — understand where we have come from and where we are going — then we must realize that humanity is now beginning to develop the ability to remember beyond the limits of the present incarnation. What matters now is that we develop it in the right way, that is, by developing our individual I. For we can remember only what we have created in our soul. If we have not created it, we are left only with the fettering memory of a group I, and we will feel this as a falling back into a group-soul of higher animality, as it were. Even if human group-souls are more refined than those of the animals, they are still group-souls. People of an earlier age would not have considered this a regression because they were just in the process of developing from group-soulness to the individual soul. However, if group-soulness is retained today, people will consciously experience this falling back into group-soulness. In the future, this will create an oppressive feeling in those who cannot catch up with the development of the individual I either in the present incarnation or a later one; they will feel their falling back into group-soulness.

Anthroposophy must help people keep pace with this development of the I; that is how we have to see anthroposophy and its place in human life. When we keep in mind that the sixth period is that of the first complete overcoming of the concept of race, we have to realize that it would be sheer fantasy to think that a sixth "race" will also start in a particular place on earth and develop like the earlier races. After all, that is what progress is all about: ever new ways of evolution appear, and concepts that were valid for earlier times will no longer apply in the future. If we do not realize this, the idea of progress will remain unclear for us. And we will again and again fall back into the error of speaking about so and so many cycles, worlds, races of evolution, and so on. It is unclear why this wheel of cycles, worlds, and races should keep turning. We must realize that the word "race" is a term that was valid only for a particular time. As we approach the sixth epoch, this term loses its meaning.

In future, what speaks to the depths of the human soul will be expressed increasingly in people's outer appearance. What people have acquired as individuals and yet experienced non-individually will be expressed in their countenance. Thus, the individuality of a person — not the group-soulness — will be inscribed on his or her countenance, and that is what will account for human diversity. Everything will be acquired individually, although it will only be gained through overcoming the individuality. Those who are in the process of developing the I will not form groups, but their individuality will be expressed in their external appearance. That is what will create differences between human beings.

There will be people who have acquired I-hood; they will be scattered over the earth, and their countenances will be very diverse. Yet, in this diversity the individual I is expressing itself even in the person's gestures. However, those who have not developed their individuality will bear the imprint of group-soulness in their countenances; that is, they can be grouped in categories that will resemble each other. That will be the outer physiognomy of our earth: the possibility will be prepared to bear one's individuality as an outer sign or to bear the outer sign of group-soulness. It is the meaning of earthly evolution for human beings to develop more and more the ability to express their inner being in their outer appearance. That is why the highest ideal of the evolution of the I, Christ Jesus, is described as follows in an ancient document: "When two become one, when the outer becomes like the inner, then human beings have attained Christ nature in themselves." That is the meaning of a certain passage in the so-called Egyptian Gospel.[3] One can understand such passages on the basis of anthroposophical wisdom.

Today we have attempted to understand the task of anthroposophy out of the depth of our insight. Next time we will consider a spiritual problem that is of special concern to the individual and that can lead us to understand our destiny and our true nature.

LECTURE TWO

The God Within and the God of Outer Revelation

MUNICH, DECEMBER 7, 1909

As YOU KNOW from the spirit of our anthroposophical work over the years, our work is not based on a striving for sensations. Instead, we want to calmly examine the facts of spiritual life that are important in our lives. It is not by speaking of what lies on the surface of daily life that we serve our age spiritually, but by gaining knowledge of life's larger connections. Our individual lives are closely connected with the great events of existence, and only when we judge our own life on the basis of the greatest phenomena of life can we assess it rightly. That is why we have tried in the last three years to deepen our fundamental views in relation to universal questions. We spent the first four years in this first seven-year cycle in the existence of the German Section of the Theosophical Society establishing our views and insights. From what you heard in the various lecture cycles, you will have realized that the lectures on the Gospels are part of the work of these last three years. Those lectures not only helped us understand the contents of the Gospels, but also showed what we can learn from them about human nature. Today, we will talk more about how the Gospels can be applied to our personal lives.

Conventional science is less and less willing to consider the Gospels historical documents about the greatest individuality ever to intervene in human evolution, Christ Jesus. The attitude toward the Gospels in the first Christian

29

centuries and even in the Middle Ages was quite different from what it has become in modern times. These days, the Gospels are indeed seen as four mutually contradictory documents, and nothing seems more natural than to ask how they can be considered historical records when they contradict each other as much as they do in giving an account of what happened in Palestine at the beginning of our era.

Now, if people did not love to overlook the most important things, their thinking would inevitably have to lead them to the following realization. They would have to admit that it does not really take much to see that the Gospels contradict each other in our modern sense of the word. One could say that even a child can see the contradictions. But we could also add that nowadays the Gospels are available to everybody, and everybody can read them. However, before the invention of printing, they were not available to all people but were read only by a few people. These few were spiritual leaders. The content of the gospels was then taught to other people in a way they could understand. Now we have to ask if those few people who read the gospels, the spiritual leaders, were really such tremendous fools that they did not realize what every child can see these days, namely, that the gospels contradict each other.

When we investigate this matter, we soon notice that people's whole world of feeling toward the Gospels was different in the past. Today it is the critical intellect, trained in outer sensory reality, that has a field day with the Gospels. It has no problem at all finding the intellectual contradictions there; this is, after all, child's play.

How, then, did those leaders of spiritual life, who were

reading the Gospels, come to terms with these contradictions? On account of the Gospels, people in ancient times had a tremendous reverence we can't even imagine today for the great Christ event. Indeed they felt that precisely because they had four Gospels they should revere and appreciate the Christ event all the more. This is because these early readers of the Gospels thought quite differently than we do today. Modern readers are no cleverer than somebody who photographs a bouquet of flowers from one angle. Then he has a picture of the bouquet and shows it around. People look at it and remember the picture, thinking they now have a clear idea of what the bouquet looked like. But then someone takes a picture of the same bouquet from another angle and gets quite a different picture. He also shows it to everyone but now people say it cannot possibly be the same bouquet because the two photographs contradict each other. And if the bouquet is photographed from all four sides, the four pictures will not be at all similar; yet they will be four pictures of the same thing.

This was how the early readers of the four Gospels felt. They believed the four Gospels are four different representations of one event, each taken from another point of view. They provide a complete picture of the event precisely because they are not alike. It is only when all four sides are combined that 'a complete idea of the event in Palestine emerges. People back then felt they had to look up to the Christ event with even more humility precisely because it was presented from four perspectives, for clearly this event is so great that it cannot be understood if it is presented from only one point of view. They felt they had to be grateful to have four Gospels describing this event from four points of view. However, they saw they had to understand how these four different points of view originated. Then they could develop an idea of what the individual can derive from the four Gospels.

What we call the Christ event is a tremendous, mighty event in the spiritual evolution of humanity. What place does that event in Palestine have in this evolution? We can say that everything humanity had previously experienced spiritually merged in this event in Palestine and from then on continued in one common stream. For example, the ancient Hebrew teaching, as it is recorded in the Old Testament, is one part of this common stream. It flowed in as the event in Palestine took place. Another stream proceeded from Zarathustra. This, too, entered into Christianity, which then flowed through the world as a kind of mainstream. Likewise, what we might call the oriental spiritual stream, which found its most significant expression in Gautama Buddha, also joined the one great mainstream. All these various streams are now contained in Christianity. You do not learn what Buddhism is nowadays from people who warm over the teachings of Buddha from 600 B.C. Those teachings have flowed into Christianity. Likewise, you do not learn what Zarathustrianism really is from people who want to explain its nature on the basis of ancient Persian documents. For the one who taught in ancient Persia what was recorded in these ancient documents has evolved further. He has let his contribution to the spiritual life of humanity flow into Christianity, and we will have to look for it there.

To get a clear picture of the facts, let us consider how these three streams, Buddhism, Zarathustrianism, and the ancient Judaic stream, flowed into Christianity. To understand how Zarathustrianism flowed in, we should remember that the individuality we call Zarathustra was the great teacher of the second post-Atlantean epoch who first taught among the ancient Persians and was then incarnated again and again. Through each incarnation he ascended higher and higher, and finally he appeared around 600 B.C. as a contemporary of Buddha. He appeared in the secret schools of the ancient Chaldean-Babylonian culture and was the teacher of Pythagoras, who had gone to Chaldea to perfect himself. Then this Zarathustra, who in 600 B.C. was known as Zarathas or Nazarathos, was reborn at the beginning of our era to parents called Joseph and Mary, as described in Saint Matthew's Gospel. This child of Joseph and Mary, the so-called Bethlehem parents, was one of the two Jesus children born at the beginning of our era. Thus, we see the individuality who was the bearer of Zarathustrianism —one of the significant streams mentioned above — transplanted to ancient Palestine.

This was not the only spiritual stream that was to revive and in a new form flow on in Christianity. Many different things had to come together to bring this about. For instance, Zarathustra had to be born in a body so organized that it was possible for him to develop further the faculties he had acquired through ascending from incarnation to incarnation. We must keep in mind that no matter how highly developed an individuality is, if it descends into an unsuitable body because it cannot find a suitable one, this individuality cannot express his or her soul-spiritual faculties because it lacks the necessary physical instruments. It takes a certain kind of brain to express such faculties as Zarathustra possessed. That is, he had to be born into a body that had inherited the qualities making it an appropriate instrument for such faculties. Thus, the Jesus child described in Saint Matthew's Gospel had to have a high soul-spiritual organization in his reincarnating I, which would allow him to have the powerful effect that was necessary, and he also had to have a perfect physical organization, which was inherited, for his soul to be born into. Zarathustra had to find a suitable physical brain.

This perfectly adapted physical organization was the contribution of the ancient Hebrews to Christianity. A suitable physical body for Zarathustra, a body with the most perfect imaginable physical instruments, had to be created in the Hebrew people through purely physical heredity. This had to be prepared far back in the past through many generations so that the right qualities were passed on and then inherited by the body that was born at the beginning of our era.

Let us look at how this life flowed into the mainstream of our present spiritual life. Just as we have seen the mission of Zarathustra in relation to Christianity, so we will now find out about the mission of the ancient Hebrews. Here I must tell you that the more spiritual-scientific research progresses, the more it has to admit that the Bible, not outer cultural history, is right. What cultural history digs up appears childish in comparison with what is written in the Bible and what only needs to be read properly to be understood. For spiritual science the Bible is more correct than historical research. For example, it is true that Judaism descended, in a sense, from a common forefather called Abraham or Abram. It is indeed absolutely correct that as we trace the generations back into the past, we come to a forefather who was endowed with very special powers by the spiritual world. What were these powers? To understand what special capabilities were given to Abraham, we must recall various things we have already spoken about here.

As we have said, when we look at ancient times, we find that people had other faculties of soul than we have today; these can be called a kind of dim clairvoyance. Back then, people could not look at the world in the self-confident, intellectual way we do, but they were able to perceive the spiritual around them, spiritual phenomena, facts, and beings. Since this seeing took place in a state of dimmed consciousness, it was like a living dream, but a dream that had a vital connection to reality. This ancient clairvoyance had to become weaker so people could develop our modern way of thinking and our intellectual culture.

Human evolution is a kind of education through which the various faculties are gradually developed. For example, in our present way of seeing, we perceive, let's say, a flower without seeing its astral body winding all around it. The ancients, however, still saw the flower and its astral body. We had to be trained in our modern perception that sees objects with the sharp contours of the intellect; this training required that the ancient clairvoyance vanish. Now, there is a certain law that prevails in spiritual evolution. According to this law, every capacity humanity acquires must have its beginning in one individuality. Faculties that are to become common to a large number of people must first appear in one person. Thus, the faculties having to do with reasoning not related to clairvoyance, with evaluating the world by measure, number, and weight — faculties that aim not at seeing into the spiritual world but at understanding sensory phenomena — were first implanted by the spiritual world in the individuality known as Abraham or Abram. He was chosen to be the first to develop the powers that are especially bound to the physical brain. It is not for nothing that Abraham is called the discoverer of arithmetic, that is, of the capability to quantify the world and calculate it according to measure and number. In a sense, he was the first of those in whose soul the ancient dreamy clairvoyance was extinguished and whose brain was prepared so that the faculty using the brain as instrument could become effective. Thus, the mission given to Abraham was a significant and profound one.

Now this faculty that had been given to Abraham in rudimentary form was to become more and more perfect. As you can imagine, everything in the world must develop, and the ability to perceive the world through the physical brain was no exception. This faculty was developed through being transmitted from Abraham to the succeeding generations. However, something different had to happen in this case than is usual when a mission is passed on from the older generation to the younger. After all, other missions, especially the greatest ones, were not connected to a physical instrument, the physical brain.

For example, let us look at Zarathustra. He gave his disciples a higher, more advanced clairvoyant vision than other people had. It was not bound to a physical instrument but was transmitted from teacher to pupil. The pupil then in turn became a teacher and gave this higher clairvoyant vision to his pupils, and so on. Abraham's mission, however, was not a teaching or method of clairvoyant perception but something bound to the brain. Thus, it could be transmitted to later generations only through physical inheritance. The mission given to Abraham depended on being transmitted physically from one generation to the next, that is, the perfected organization of Abraham's brain had to be inherited by his descendants generation after generation. Because Abraham's mission consisted in perfecting the physical brain, the latter became more and more perfect from generation to generation. In other words, the mission of Abraham depended on procreation for its gradual perfection in the course of physical evolution.

There was yet something else connected with this contribution of the ancient Hebrew people, and we will understand what it was when we consider people in other civilizations who had dim clairvoyance. We can ask how they received what was most important to them, what they revered most in all the world. They received it as inspirations that lit up within them. They did not have to do research as we do. Nowadays, we establish sciences by investigating the world outside us, by experimenting and deducing laws from the external facts. The ancients did not gain their knowledge in this way; rather, it lit up within them as an inspiration like a flash of lightning. They received their knowledge in their inner being; their souls had to give birth to it within them. They had to turn their gaze away from the outer world in order to allow the highest truths to blossom forth within them as inspirations.

This was to become different for those who derived their mission from Abraham. Abraham had to bring to humanity precisely the results of observation and reasoning. When people in those civilizations that were built on ancient clairvoyance looked up to the highest, they felt, "I am grateful to the God who reveals himself to me within me. I turn my gaze away from the outer world, and the Godhead is most present to me when, without looking at the outside world, I let his inspirations light up within me."

However, the descendants of Abraham were to

renounce inspirations coming from within themselves and prepare themselves to turn their gaze to the world around them. They were to observe what is revealed in air and water, in mountain and plain, and in the starry world, and to ponder how all things exist side by side. They were to connect external things with one another and to gain an all-embracing thought from this. When they condensed what they saw in the outer world into one single thought, they called what the outer world told them Yahweh or Jehovah. They were to receive the highest through a revelation that speaks through the outer world.

In contrast to what other peoples were to contribute, the mission of the Abrahamic people was to give humanity what came as revelation from outside. Therefore, the instrument of spiritual life had to be inherited so that its organization was appropriate for the revelations from outside, just as earlier the inner powers of soul had to be adapted to the revelations from within.

Let us look at what happened when the clairvoyants of ancient times yielded to revelations from within themselves. They turned their gaze away from the outer world because what was revealed there could tell them nothing about the spiritual world. They even turned their gaze away from the sun and stars and listened only to what was within. There, a great inspiration about the secrets of the world was revealed, and they had a picture of the structure of the cosmos. What these ancient clairvoyants knew about the stars and their movements, about the laws of the starry world, and about the spiritual worlds was not acquired through external observation. Rather, the ancients knew something about Mars, Saturn, and so on because they had revealed themselves within these people. The laws of the universe, which are inscribed in the stars, were also inscribed within the human soul and revealed themselves there in inspirations. Just as the laws of the universe, which rule the stars, were revealed in the soul, so the laws that rule the world were now to be revealed to the Abrahamic people through outer reasoning and deduction — that is, those laws had to be grasped through outer revelation.

For this purpose, heredity had to be guided in such a way that the brain could acquire the qualities enabling it to perceive the right relationships between things. This wonderful lawfulness was implanted into the predispositions transmitted to Abraham, predispositions that developed through the generations in such a way that their organization corresponds to the great cosmic laws. The brain had to be transmitted so that its inner capabilities and its structure developed like the laws of numbers in the stars in the universe. This is why Jehovah said to Abraham, "You will see generations descend from you that will be ordered and arranged in accordance with the numbers of the stars in the heavens." The generations following Abraham were to be arranged in harmonious numerical relationships just as the stars in the sky are ordered in harmonious relations. In other words, these generations were to bear within them laws that are like the laws of the stars in the heavens.

In the heavens, there are twelve constellations. An image of this was to appear in the twelve tribes of descendants of Abraham so that the faculties that were implanted in rudimentary form in Abraham could be carried down through the generations. In the organic structure of this people, developing further from age to age, an image was to be created of number and measure in the heavens. In one Bible translation this is rendered as, "I will multiply your descendants as the stars of heaven and as the sand which is on the seashore." In truth, however, the passage should read, "Your descendants shall be grouped regularly in their blood relationships so that their arrangement is an image of the laws of the stars in the heavens." The Bible is profound, but the way it is presented these days is colored by the modern view of the world. Thus, we read, "I will multiply your descendants as the stars of heaven and as the sand which is on the seashore," while a true translation would be, "Your descendants shall be so regularly grouped that, for example, twelve tribes will arise that correspond to the twelve constellations."

Thus, the individual characteristics had to express that the Abrahamic people was to realize that their mission was a gift from outside, not something that came to life within them. They had to know that what they have to bring to the world is given to them from the outside. The Bible wonderfully expresses that Abraham's mission comes to him from outside in contrast to the old revelations that were given from within. What was this mission? Abraham's mission was to provide what flows through the blood up to the time of Christ Jesus. The entire spirituality of a certain stream had to be placed into this. It was to work as if it came as a gift from outside. Abraham had to give to the world the ancient Hebrew people. That was his mission.

If this people was to be in keeping with this mission, it had to be given to Abraham as a gift from outside. Abraham had a son, Isaac, and he was asked to sacrifice this son, as the Bible tells us. As Abraham was about to carry out the sacrifice, his son was given back to him by Jehovah. What was Abraham given there? The entire Hebrew people descended from Isaac. If Isaac had been sacrificed, it would not have come into being. Thus, the whole Hebrew people was given to Abraham as a gift. The sparing of Isaac wonderfully expresses the nature of this gift. It was Abraham's mission to father the Hebrew people, and with Isaac he received it as a gift from Jehovah.

This is how profound the stories in the Bible are; all of them correspond in their impressive details to the inner character of the progressive development of humanity. The Old Testament Hebrews gradually had to relinquish the ancient clairvoyance that continued within the other civilizations. This clairvoyance was connected to faculties coming from the spiritual world, which were designated according to their nature by expressions taken from the names for the constellations. The last faculty to be given up in exchange for the gift of the Hebrew people was connected with the sign of the Ram. Therefore, a ram was sacrificed in place of Isaac. This is the external expression of the sacrifice of the last clairvoyant power, making it possible for Abraham to receive the Hebrew people as a gift. The Hebrews were chosen to develop the faculties for observation of the outer world. Nevertheless, every new development contains also atavistic remnants of earlier things. That is why everything that was not purely in the blood and still recalled ancient clairvoyance had to be excluded for the sake of the transmission of the new outer-directed faculties. Thus, the Hebrews always had to exclude what came as an inheritance from other peoples.

We come now to a subject that is difficult to discuss because it contains a truth far removed from modern thinking. Nevertheless, it is a truth, and those who have worked for a while in anthroposophical groups may be able to accept a truth that is foreign to the conventional modern thinking. We must be aware that certain classes of people in ancient times retained their earlier faculties into later ages, especially faculties related to knowing. Clairvoyant powers lived in human souls, and people were closely connected with spiritual beings who revealed themselves in their souls. In certain people, who were the products of the decline of these ancient times, there developed ultimately a lower form of this connection to the spiritual world around them. While the actual clairvoyants were connected with the whole universe through spiritual intuition and inspiration, those who were part of the process of decline and who developed this connection to the spiritual in a phase of decadence were actually lower types of people. They were not independent because their I was undeveloped, and at the same time their clairvoyant faculties were already declining. Such individuals appeared throughout history, and in them we can see the relationship between certain physical organs and the clairvoyant organs.

Now we arrive at the truth that will sound strange to you. What we call ancient clairvoyance, this lighting up of the cosmic secrets within human souls, had to enter the soul somehow. We have to picture this as streams flowing into human beings. The ancients did not perceive them, but when these streams had occurred and lit up within them, people perceived them as their inspirations. In other words, certain streams flowed into people from their environment; in later periods these streams were transformed. In the distant past, these streams were purely spiritual, and clairvoyants could perceive them as purely astral-etheric streams. But later these purely spiritual streams dried up, as it were, and condensed to etheric-physical streams. What became of them? They developed into hair. Our hair is the result of these ancient streams. The hair on our body was formerly spiritual streams that flowed from outside into human beings. Our hair is nothing else but dried up astral-etheric streams.

Such facts are preserved only where the old truths have been retained externally in writing or through tradition. In Hebrew the characters for the words "hair" and "light" are approximately the same because people were conscious of the kinship between the light streaming in astrally and hair. In general, the greatest truths are contained in ancient Hebrew literature in the words themselves.

So, we can say human evolution is progressive. However, in those people whose ancient faculties were declining the incoming streams changed and dried up, but no new faculties appeared to take their place. Those people were connected with the new in an old way, yet unconnected because the streams were dried up. Such people were very hairy, while those who developed further were less hairy because new powers replaced those that later condensed into hair.

It will take a long time for science to arrive at these significant truths. Nevertheless, they can be found in the Bible. The Bible is far wiser than our science, which is still at the stage of a child beginning to learn his ABC's. Read the story of Jacob and Esau. Jacob was the one who progressed a step further and developed the new faculty; Esau, on the other hand, remained at an earlier stage, and compared to Jacob he was a simpleton. When they were presented to their father Isaac, their mother had covered Jacob with false hair to make Isaac confuse his younger son with Esau. This shows us that the Old Testament Hebrews still had retained something that was inherited from other cultures and that had to be discarded. Esau is cast out, and what was to live on as sense-based reasoning is transmitted through Jacob. Here, what had remained in a retarded form was expelled in Esau. Similarly, the ancient clairvoyant faculties, an atavistic inheritance, appeared in Joseph, who was consequently expelled by his brothers to Egypt. Joseph had dreams through which he could interpret the world — this faculty was not to be developed in the mission of the Abrahamic people. Therefore, Joseph was cast out and had to go to Egypt.

There we see how a stream evolved in the Hebrew people that is built on the blood relationships of generations and from which the remnants of the old inheritance are gradually expelled. It was the special faculty of the ancient Hebrews to turn what is inherited down through the generations into a more and more perfect instrument so that finally a body could be produced that could be the instrument for Christ who would incarnate in it. If the Hebrews could no longer receive revelations from within, they had to receive them from without. They had to receive through external revelation even those things other peoples received through direct inspiration. That is, the Jews, led by Joseph, had to go to a people that still possessed the old inspiration. There, Joseph was initiated into the Egyptian mysteries, and the Jews attained through external means the knowledge they needed about the spiritual worlds. They even received their moral laws from the outside rather than as something lighting up within them. After they had assimilated what they had to take in from outside, they returned to Palestine.

We must now show how the Hebrews gradually developed from generation to generation so that finally the body of Jesus could be produced, and the ancient Hebrew stream flow into Christianity. Remember our discussion of the development of rudimentary characteristics in individuals. The life of an individual can be divided into periods of seven years. The first period, in which the physical body simply builds its forms, extends from birth to the change of teeth at the age of seven. The second period, in which the etheric body is active in growth and forming, continues until puberty. The forms are defined until the age of seven and the already-defined forms are then enlarged. From fourteen to twenty-one the astral body is especially predominant, and at twenty-one the true I is born and becomes independent. The life of the individual runs its course in certain periods until the birth of the human I.

In the same way the gifts of the people that was to provide a body for the most perfect I had to develop gradually. What takes place over years in an individual, however, develops in a people over generations. Each successive generation must further develop the characteristics of the preceding one. To explain the occult reasons for this would lead us too far afield, but you might recall a quite ordinary phenomenon. Just remember that certain qualities are inherited not directly, but skip a generation. For example, it is the grandson who resembles the grandfather in those characteristics. It was the same in the inheritance of qualities in successive generations of the Hebrews; every other generation was skipped.

What is one period of seven years in an individual's life corresponds in the successive generations of a people to two periods or fourteen generations. We can therefore say the Hebrews developed in twice seven or fourteen generations, which corresponds to the period from birth to the change

of teeth in the individual. The following period corresponds to that between the change of teeth and puberty and
again comprises twice seven generations. A third period of
twice seven generations corresponds to the years between
fourteen and twenty-one, when the astral body is especially
prominent. It was then possible for the I to be born in the
Hebrew people after three times twice seven or three times
fourteen, that is, forty-two generations.

To describe the body that became Zarathustra's instrument, I had to show how the seed given to Abraham
developed through thrice fourteen generations so that the I
could be born, just as in the individual the I is born into the
threefold corporeality after thrice seven years. The writer of
Saint Matthew's Gospel shows this. He describes thrice
fourteen generations — the generations from Abraham to
David, from David to the Babylonian Captivity, and from
the Babylonian Captivity to the birth of Jesus. Here, from
the profundity of knowledge Saint Matthew's Gospel
points to the mission of the Hebrews, showing how the
forces were gradually developed that made it possible for
the perfect I attained by Zarathustra to be born in a body
produced by this people.

Looking at the destiny of the Hebrews, we find that the
Babylonian Captivity occurred at the period when the
individual, after the age of fourteen, prepares for life, when
the hopes of youth to be realized later take root. The
Babylonian Captivity was the time when the astral body of
the Hebrews developed, and what gives this astral body its
impulse in the final fourteen generations of the forty-two
was implanted into it then. That is why the Hebrews were
led into the Babylonian Captivity where, six hundred years
before our era, Zarathas or Nazarathos was incarnated as

the teacher in the Mystery schools of the Babylonians. There, the most prominent Hebrew leaders came in contact with Zarathas, the great teacher of that era. Zarathas joined them and became their teacher. From him the Hebrew leaders received the impulse that, in their last fourteen generations, prepared them for the birth of Jesus.

History as we know it then unfolded, and we see the writer of Saint Matthew's Gospel take into account a law in the spiritual sphere that will be recognized more and more as significant for all life. This is the law that whatever has happened earlier is repeated at a higher stage. This is expressed in science in a somewhat distorted form in the axiom that what occurs at a lower stage of the species throughout long epochs is repeated in brief in each individual. The writer of Saint Matthew's Gospel shows this in a magnificent way by saying that the I of Zarathustra was to incarnate in a body that was gradually developed within the Abrahamic people.

Abraham proceeded from Ur in Chaldea, the place where Babylonian civilization originated, through Asia Minor to Palestine. Through the dreams of Joseph, his descendants were led farther south to Egypt, and after they had received the Egyptian impulse, they returned to Canaan. This was the fate of the whole people. First, they were led through Canaan to Egypt, and then back again to Canaan. This fate of the whole people was to be repeated in brief. After all that had originated in Abraham had been developed, after the sheaths had been prepared, Zarathustra's I again took Chaldea as its point of departure. His spirit was connected with Chaldea, and in his last incarnation he was the Mystery teacher there.

What path does Zarathustra's soul take when it incarnates in Bethlehem? He had remained connected with the Magi, who had been initiated in the Chaldean Mystery schools. They remembered that they had heard him say he would reappear and that his soul, which had always been called "the golden star," would proceed at a particular time to Bethlehem. When the time came, they followed the path his soul took, thus repeating the path of the Old Testament Hebrews. As Abraham traveled the road to Canaan, so this star, the soul of Zarathustra, also followed it. The three Magi followed the star of Zarathustra, and he led them to the place where he was born into the body from the Abrahamic people that was destined for him. Thus, the I of Zarathustra repeated in spirit the path Abraham had taken to Palestine.

The Old Testament Hebrews then had to seek the way to Egypt. They were led there by Joseph's dreams. Now the I that was born in the Jesus-child of Bethlehem was led through the dreams of another Joseph to Egypt along the same path the Abrahamic people had followed earlier. Zarathustra's I repeated in Jesus' body the ancient Hebrews' destiny, going first to Egypt and then returning to Palestine. Here, we have a recapitulation in spirit through the I of Zarathustra, reflecting the earlier fate of the Hebrews.

Based on his knowledge of the spiritual law that what appears at a higher stage is a brief repetition of what has occurred earlier, the writer of Saint Matthew's Gospel faithfully describes all this. How profoundly these Gospels record the event that inaugurated our era! That event is so great that the four evangelists found that each of them could only describe it from his own standpoint. Each of them has described this event according to his own limited powers. When we see someone from one of four sides, we get only one picture, and only by combining mutually contradictory pictures do we get an overall idea of the person. Similarly, the writer of Saint Matthew's Gospel described what he knew through initiation about the law of thrice twice seven, the law of forty-two, and about the preparation of the body for the great I of Jesus of Nazareth. Through his initiation, the writer of this gospel knew the Mysteries according to which Jesus's body was prepared as the mission of the Hebrews. The writer of Saint Luke's Gospel described, on the basis of his initiation, how the stream of the Buddha flowed into Christianity. The other evangelists have described the event on the basis of their initiations. The event they recorded is so profound that we must be grateful to find it described from the point of view of four initiates.

Today I just wanted to mention a few details of the spiritual origin of Christianity to show how our knowledge of the world and of humanity grows when we study this greatest of human events. I wanted to give you an idea of how deeply this event should be taken and how profound the Gospels really are when we know how to read them.

LECTURE THREE

The Lord of the Soul

MUNICH, DECEMBER 12, 1910

MANY OF THE lectures I have given over the years in anthroposophical groups to friends — some of whom are sitting here today — have dealt with the gospels of John, Luke, and Matthew.[1] In those lectures, we have tried to recreate in our minds the great event in Palestine, the Mystery of Golgotha, from three different angles — in three different ways, so to speak. We hope these lectures could establish an ever-increasing appreciation of this unique event in our souls. I have already pointed out that we have four gospels because their authors were inspired occultists and each wanted to represent this great event from one perspective only, just as we take pictures or photograph external objects from only one point of view. When we then take the pictures from various angles and combine them, looking at all of them together, we can have the actual reality before our souls. Thus, each of the evangelists gives us the opportunity to consider the great event of Palestine from one particular standpoint.

The Gospel of Saint John gives us an insight into these events from a perspective we may call a revelation of the highest human and occult aims, as well as of the highest world principle. In Saint Luke's Gospel, on the other hand, we are given an insight into the secrets surrounding the personality of Jesus of Nazareth — the Solomon and Nathan Jesuses — up to the moment when his inspiration through the Christ took place. As you know from my

51

lecture cycle on the Gospel of Saint Matthew — if you missed the lectures you can read them later — this gospel shows how the physical body in which Christ was to be incarnated for three years was prepared in the Hebrew people.

In a certain way, the Gospel of Saint Mark leads us to the highest summits of the spiritual-scientific, Christian world view. It gives us the opportunity to look into many things that are imparted to us through the gospels but are not touched upon in the same way by the other evangelists. Today, therefore, I have set myself the task to speak about this gospel.

We must be aware that it is necessary to consider many things that the superficial world of our time does not really want to look at. If we want to understand Saint Mark's Gospel in all its depth, we must familiarize ourselves with the different way of expressing things that prevailed at the time when Christ Jesus walked the earth. Do not take it amiss, then, if in order to convey what I have to tell you, I paint it in strong colors.

We express what we want to say in language, which is to bring out what lives in our souls. The expression of soul content in language differs from one epoch of human development to another. In the Hebraic epoch, the ancient Hebrew sacred language provided a wonderful way of expressing things. It was very different from our way of clothing the secrets of the soul into words. When a word was spoken in old Hebrew, it contained not merely an abstract idea, as it does today, but a whole world. The vowels were not written because the speaker expressed his innermost being through his way of vocalizing, whereas the consonants contained the description — the picture, so to speak — of what was outside. We can say that when the Hebrews wrote, for example, what corresponds to our *B*, they always felt something like a picture of outer conditions, something that formed a warm, hutlike enclosure. The letter *B* always evoked the image of something that can enclose a being like a house; the letter could not be pronounced without this image living in the speaker's soul. When *A* was vocalized, there was always something of strength and force, even of radiating power, living within it. That is how the soul lived on; the spiritual-psychological content flowed out with the words, soared into space, and touched other souls. Obviously, language was then a far more living affair and entered more fully into the secrets of existence than our contemporary language.

That is the light in the picture I mentioned. The shadows are in our having become, to a great extent, philistines. Our language expresses only abstractions and generalities, and we no longer even notice this — so our language at bottom expresses only the philistine. It could not be otherwise in an age when people begin to write literature long before they have any spiritual content to express, when an infinite amount of printed material goes to the general public, when everyone thinks he must write something, and when everything can be a subject to write about. I have even seen authors turning up at the founding of our society out of curiosity, hoping to find material for a novel in it and looking for protagonists that can be dished up in the popular style.

We must be aware, then, that our language has become abstract, empty, and philistine, in contrast to the way it was when people still thought of language as something holy, something that must be handled responsibly, and through which God would speak. That is why it is so infinitely difficult to squeeze the tremendous facts imparted to us by, and resounding in, the gospels into modern words. Why shouldn't people these days believe that everything can be expressed in contemporary language? They cannot understand that this language is empty of what even the Greeks expressed with one word. Furthermore, reading the Bible today, we find something that, compared to its original content, has been sifted once, twice, even thrice, but in such a way that not the best but only the worst remains. It is therefore rather cheap to refer to the modern wording of the Bible. We go most astray, however, when we turn to the Gospel of Mark as we have it in the Bible today.

In the translation by Weizsäcker, which is generally considered excellent — and because it is considered so excellent nowadays, we can assume that it is not all that good — the first lines of the Gospel of St. Mark are rendered as follows:

> As it is written in the prophet Isaiah, behold,
> I send my messenger before thee, who shall pre-
> pare the way for thee; listen how it calls in the
> wilderness, prepare the way of the Lord, make
> straight his paths.

Honest people must really admit that if Weizsäcker begins the Gospel of Saint Mark like this, they do not understand a single word of it; those who claim to understand this are fooling themselves. People who work honestly will not be able to understand the lines, "Behold, I send my messenger before thy face, who shall prepare thy way; the voice of one crying in the wilderness: Prepare the way of the Lord, make his paths straight." For they express either a triviality or something that cannot be understood. The concepts that make it possible to understand what Isaiah says here must first be acquired. For Isaiah pointed to the great, tremendous event that was to be the most significant event in human evolution. What was he really referring to?

Based upon what we already know, we can say what Isaiah prophesied. We can say that in ancient times humanity had a kind of clairvoyance that allowed people to grow into the divine-spiritual world with their soul forces. But what really happened when people grew thus into the spiritual world? They ceased to make use of the I, insofar as they had developed it at that time. Instead, they used their astral body, with its forces of vision and seership — whereas the forces rooted in the I were gradually awakened in the process of perceiving the physical world. It is the I that uses the senses as instruments. When the ancients sought enlightenment about the world, they employed their astral bodies. They saw and perceived in their astral bodies. Further evolution consisted in the transition from the use of the astral body to the use of the I. In regard to the I, the Christ impulse was the most intense impulse. If Christ is taken into the I in the sense of St. Paul's words, "It is no longer I who live, but Christ who lives in me," then the I will have the power to grow into the spiritual world through its own efforts. Formerly, only the astral body could do this.

Thus, we can say of human evolution that human beings formerly used their astral body as an organ of perception, but gradually lost the ability to develop organs of perception in the astral body. As humanity approached the time of the Christ event, it entered an evolutionary stage in which people had to realize that their astral body was less and less able to see into the spiritual world. The astral body's connection to the spiritual world came to nothing, and the I was not yet forceful enough to get any enlightenment from the outer world. That was the time when Christ drew near.

Now in the evolution of humanity, certain great steps forward are gradually prepared before they actually take place. This was the case with the Christ impulse, but there had to be a transition. The development I just described could not have gone so far that human beings would have seen their astral body gradually becoming dulled toward the spiritual world and would have felt an utter desolation and dreariness in themselves until the I would have been kindled later through the Christ impulse. Things were not to turn out that way. Rather, a few individuals developed so far that through a particular influence from the spiritual world they saw with the astral body something similar to what people were to see and know later through the I. In other words, the I was prepared in the astral body.

Indeed, it is through the I and its development that human beings have become earthly beings. The astral body really belonged to the ancient moon when the angels, the Angeloi, were at the human stage. The angels were human on the old moon; we are human beings on the earth. On the old moon, human beings appropriately used their astral body, and everything else was just preparation for the evolution of the I. The beginning of our earth evolution was a repetition of our moon evolution on a higher level. After all, had we remained limited to the astral body, we could never have become fully human. Only angels on the moon could become human in the astral body. Therefore, just as Christ lived in earthly human beings in order to inspire the I in them, so for the preparation of the I there had to be prophets from the angels of the moon, the moon-humans, to inspire the astral body so that the I-hood of human beings could be prepared. A prophet could have characterized it in the following way. "There will come a time in human evolution when humanity will be ripe for the development of the I. Only the angels of the moon were raised to the highest in their astral bodies, but for human beings to be prepared for this I-hood, certain people on earth had to be so inspired through grace and under exceptional conditions that they could work as angels even though they were humans. They were angels in human form."

Here we arrive at an important occult concept that is indispensable to the occult understanding of human evolution. It is naturally easy to say that all is Maya, but that is an abstraction. We must really take it seriously and be able to say, "A human being stands before me, but he or she is Maya. Who knows, he or she may not really be human. Perhaps the humanness is only an outer veil employed by quite another being, not a human one, to bring about something that cannot yet be effected by humanity." I have indicated something of this in my *Portal of Initiation*.[2]

Such an event occurred when the individuality who lived in Elijah was reborn in John the Baptist. An angel entered his soul and used his body and soul to do what would have been impossible for a human being to accomplish. An angel lived in John who had to announce the true I that was to live in Jesus of Nazareth. It is extremely important to know that John the Baptist is only Maya and that an angelic messenger lived in him. This is found also in the Greek version of the Bible: "Behold, I send my messenger [i.e., Angeloi or angel]." Thus, a profound cosmic mystery connected with John the Baptist was prophesied by Isaiah. As we have seen, Isaiah characterized John as Maya or illusion, but in truth John encompassed the angel who had to announce what humanity really was to become through receiving the Christ impulse. Angels proclaim beforehand what humanity is to become later. So, this passage in the Bible should really read, "Behold, what gives I-hood to the world sends the angel before thee to whom I-hood will be given."

Now we go on to the third sentence. What does it mean? Here we must call to mind the whole historical world situation. What happened after the astral body gradually lost the ability to extend its forces like tentacles to look clairvoyantly into the spiritual world? Formerly, when the astral body became active, it could see into the spiritual world. This possibility gradually disappeared, and it became dark within human beings. While they could spread their astral body over all the beings of the spiritual world in former times, now they were alone in themselves. Their souls now lived in solitude. That also is in the Greek text. "Behold, what speaks in the solitude — or, if you like, wilderness — of the soul when the astral body could no longer extend out to the divine spiritual world. Listen to what calls in the wilderness and loneliness of the soul."

What is it that announces itself? Here, we must be clear about the meaning of one particular word when it is used in reference to spiritual or soul phenomena. This was true, above all, in Hebrew, but also in Greek. The word is *Kyrios*. To translate it as "the Lord," as is usually done, produces absolute nonsense. What does this word mean? In ancient times everyone who spoke this word knew it meant something that was connected with the progress of the human soul. People knew that the word *Kyrios* referred to secrets of the soul.

Looking at the astral body, we see that our soul has three distinct forces we call thinking, feeling, and willing. The soul thinks, feels, and wills. These are the three forces working in the soul. They are the serving forces in the soul. Formerly, they had been the lords of humanity, and human beings had been subject to them and had to wait for their thinking, feeling, or willing to be called into action. As human beings evolved, however, these soul forces became subject to the Kyrios, the Lord of the soul forces, the I. When the term *Kyrios* referred to the soul, nothing else was understood by it than the I. This I no longer believed that the divine spiritual thinks, feels, and wills in it, but "*I* think, *I* feel, *I* will." The Lord makes himself felt in the forces of the soul. "Prepare yourselves, you human souls, to follow paths that lead you to let the strong I — Kyrios, the Lord —awaken in your souls. Listen to the call in the solitude of the soul. Prepare the force or direction of the Lord of the soul — the I. Make open his forces!" That is roughly how this passage should be translated. "Open up, so that the I can enter and does not become the slave of thinking, feeling, and willing. Open up its forces!" When you translate these words, "Behold, the I sends its angel before you that is to give you the possibility of understanding the calls in the solitude of the astral soul: Prepare the directions of the I, and open the forces for it," you then have a meaning in these significant words of the prophet Isaiah and a reference to the greatest event in human evolution. You then understand that Isaiah speaks of John the Baptist, that he points out that our soul solitude longs for the approach of the Lord in the soul, the approach of the I. The words have force and weight only when we understand them this way.

Why was John the Baptist able to be the bearer of the Angeloi? He could do this because he had had a certain initiation. Each initiation is specialized. Initiations are not just general, but specialized. Individuals who have a very special task need a particular kind of initiation. Now for everything that occurs in the spiritual world precautions have been taken so that the starry script in the heavens reveals spiritual facts. For example, people could have a sun-initiation and enter into the secrets of the spiritual world that is the realm of Ahura Mazdao, the world for which the sun is the external expression. There are, however, twelve different ways to be initiated into the secrets of the sun; each of these initiations was a "solar initiation," yet different from the other eleven. Depending upon what a person has to accomplish for humanity, he or she receives an initiation that can be described as a solar initiation but, for example, one where the forces flow in as though the sun were standing in Cancer. This differs from the initiation where the forces flow in as though the sun were standing in Libra. This is how different specialized initiations were designated.

Individuals who have as important a mission as John the Baptist must be initiated in a very special way. Only then will they have the necessary strength to accomplish their mission in the world even in a rather single-minded way if circumstances require that. So, in order for John the Baptist to become the bearer of the Angeloi, he had to undergo the sun-initiation that can be called the initiation in the sign of Aquarius. The sun in Aquarius is a symbol for the initiation John the Baptist received to become the bearer of the angel. He received the force of the sun as it streams down when its relation to the other stars is characterized with the words, "The sun stands in the constellation of Aquarius." That was the symbol. John had undergone the Aquarius initiation.

The constellation was given the name Aquarius because those who underwent this initiation had the power to do with human beings what John did as the Aquarian, the Baptist. Through immersion in water, he brought people to the point where their etheric bodies were freed sufficiently for them to gain the self-knowledge that allowed them to realize what was most important in their time. People were immersed and their etheric bodies were freed for a moment. Through baptism in the Jordan, people could feel the special importance of this epoch in the history of the world. Therefore, John underwent the baptism initiation. To express symbolically the flowing in of the rays from the constellation in which the sun stood, this sign was called Aquarius. In this way the name of the human capacity is carried over to the heavens.

Today many learned ignoramuses try to interpret spiritual events by bringing the heavens down to earth. They say, "Now, that indicates a forward movement of the sun." These learned people, who really do not know anything, interpret human events from the heavens. However, it was the other way around. What lives in humanity spiritually was transferred to the heavens; the heavens were used as a means of expression. Thus, John the Baptist could say, "I have baptized you with water," which was the same as saying, "I baptize you with water: I am endowed with the initiation of Aquarius." That is what John could have said to his closest disciples. With our senses we see the constellation of Virgo opposite Aquarius, and from there the sun moves to Libra. However, in terms of initiation, the sun proceeds in the opposite direction, not as it appears to our senses. Thus, we have to look at the sun's path from Aquarius to Pisces. John could say, "Something will come that will no longer work in the way that corresponds to the sun's influence in Aquarius; instead, it will work in a way corresponding to the sun's effect in Pisces. One will come who will bring a higher baptism."

When the spiritual sun rises higher, then the Aquarian baptism becomes a baptism with spiritual water. The sun ascends in the spiritual realm from Aquarius to Pisces, hence the well-known ancient fish symbol for the bearer of Christ. Through special spiritual influences, John had an Aquarian initiation. But the initiation that came about mysteriously through the Mysteries around Jesus, of which I have spoken several times, was a Pisces initiation. It resulted from the sun advancing to the next constellation, and Jesus of Nazareth was integrated into his time through being subjected first to a Pisces initiation.

This is sufficiently indicated in the Gospel of Saint Mark, but such things can only be shown in images. Christ Jesus draws together all those who are fishing, so his first apostles are all fishermen. The advancing of the sun from Aquarius to Pisces is obvious when John tells us, "I have baptized you with water; but he will baptize you with the Holy Spirit." When Christ walked along the Sea of Galilee — which means, when the sun was so far advanced that one could see its counterpart coming up from Pisces — the fishermen Simon, Simon's brother, James, and James's brother, were inspired. This can be understood only when we look more closely at the way people expressed things at that time.

Our modern way of expressing ourselves is pedantic. If a person stands before us, we say there is a human being. If a second person stands before us, we again say there is a human being. A third, another, and so on, but we have merely Maya before us. If a being has two legs and a human countenance, then in our pedantic way of expressing ourselves we have only one term, "human being." However, what is a human being to occultism? Nothing but Maya! He or she is about the same as a rainbow, which lasts only so long as the necessary relationships between rain and sunshine exist. When these relationships change, the rainbow disappears.

It is the same with human beings. A human being is only the streaming together of forces of the macrocosm, forces we find in the heavens, here or there in the macrocosm. Where we usually assume a human being somewhere on earth, there is nothing for the occultist. In fact, forces stream down from above and up from below and intersect. Then, just as the peculiar relationship of rain and sunshine produces the rainbow, so forces streaming out of the macrocosm from above and below result in the phenomenon that looks like a human being. People are nothing as they stand before us. In truth, they are a phantom, Maya, an illusion. It is the cosmic forces, intersecting where our eyes think they see a human being, that are real. Try to take the statement seriously that a human being is nothing as he or she stands before us. A human being is but the shadow of many forces. The being who reveals himself in a person can easily be elsewhere than at that point where the individual in question is walking around on two legs.

For example, consider three men, first, an ancient Persian whose work was plowing. He looked like an ordinary man but actually was one of the souls whose forces were nourished from this or that world, above or below. The second man was an ancient Persian official. He was formed by forces from another world that intersected in him. To know him, we must look at these forces. All of you sitting here are in your reality somewhere else, and only the forces of your real being radiate into this room. Our third example is a Persian of whom we have to say he was really a complete illusion, a phantom. What was there in reality? We must go all the way up to the sun to find the forces that nourished this phantom. There, among the mysteries of the sun, we find what can be called the Golden Star, Zarathustra. It radiates down, and here below stands a figure called Zarathustra. In truth, however, his being is not there at all. This is our third example.

Now, it is important to realize that in ancient times people were aware of the meaning of such designations. Names were not given as they are today. People were named according to what lived in them rather than on the basis of their external, illusory appearance. We must be quite clear about this. We can say that at the time of Christ people would have easily understood what was meant when John the Baptist was referred to as the angel of God. Such a statement would have taken account of what really happened there; it would have focused on the main thing and disregarded secondary considerations.

Let us assume people had spoken about Christ Jesus in the same way. How would they have had to speak of him if they had understood such things? They would not have dreamt of naming the physical body walking around among them Christ Jesus. Rather, the name was the sign that what was streaming down spiritually from the sun was received in a very special way at the point where this physical body was. As this body of Jesus wandered from one place to another, it made visible the sun force as it moves from place to place. This force could also move around alone, and at times it was said that Christ Jesus was in his "home," that is, in his physical body, but what was in him moved on without his body. Particularly in Saint John's Gospel this expression is used in such a way that, at times, the writer speaks of this being moving purely spiritually exactly as though he were describing this sun force dwelling in a physical body.

It is therefore important that the deeds of Christ Jesus are always seen in relation to the physical sun, which is the external expression of the spiritual world that is received at the point where Christ's physical body is walking around. When Christ Jesus heals, for instance, it is the sun force that heals. However, the sun must be at the right place in the heavens: "That evening, at sundown, they brought to him all who were sick or possessed with demons." It is important to indicate that this healing power can flow down only when the external sun has set but still works spiritually. And when Christ again needed a certain force for his work, he had to take it from the spiritual rather than from the physical, visible sun. "And in the morning, a great while before day, he rose and went out to a lonely place, and there he prayed." Here, the path of the sun and the solar force is expressly indicated. It is this solar force that is at work here, and fundamentally Jesus is only the external sign, making the path of the sun forces visible to the physical eye.

Whenever Christ is mentioned in Saint Mark's Gospel, the sun force is meant, which, in that epoch of human evolution, was especially active in Palestine. The sun force could be seen as Christ went from one place to another. We could just as well say that at that time, the spiritual force of the sun, as though focused in one point, went from one place to another. The body of Jesus was the external sign that made the movements of the sun force visible. The paths Jesus took in Palestine were those of the sun force come down to earth. If you trace his steps on a map, you have a diagram of a cosmic event: the influence of the sun force from the macrocosm on the land of Palestine. That macrocosmic aspect is what matters here. The writer of Saint Mark's Gospel points out this macrocosmic connection. He knew that the body serving as the vehicle of a principle such as that of Christ had to be overcome by its principle in a special way. Thus, this gospel points to the world whose existence behind the world of the senses Zarathustra had so powerfully announced; it points to that world as it works on our human world. Through Christ Jesus it was indicated how these forces now work on the earth. Therefore, a kind of repetition of the Zarathustra events had to occur in the body of the Nathan Jesus because it was in a certain way influenced by the individuality of Zarathustra.

Let us recall the beautiful legend about Zarathustra. At his birth, Zarathustra accomplished his first miracle when he showed his famous smile. Later, Duransarun, the king of the district where Zarathustra was born, resolved to murder him because of what some retrograde Magi had told him about the child. However, when the king attempted to stab the child, his arm was paralyzed. That was a second miracle. Then, because the king could not stab him, Zarathustra was left among the wild beasts of the desert. Thus, in earliest childhood Zarathustra experienced what we see when we look out into the world through our impurities. Instead of noble group-soul and higher spiritual beings, we see emanations of our wild fantasy. That is what is meant when we are told that Zarathustra was left among the wild beasts, but remained unharmed. That is the third miracle. The fourth occurred also among the wild animals, and so on. It was always the good spirit of Ahura Mazdao who served Zarathustra and ministered to him.

We find these miracles repeated in the Gospel of Saint Mark. "The Spirit immediately drove him out into the wilderness [Actually the word is solitude]. And he was in the wilderness forty days, tempted by Satan; and he was with the wild beasts; and the angels ministered to him." This shows us that the body was prepared that was to be the focal point to receive what transpired in the macrocosm. What had happened to Zarathustra had to be repeated, among other things, the time he spent among the wild beasts. This body took in what came from the macrocosm.

Even the first lines of Saint Mark's Gospel take us into the greatest cosmic context. I wanted to show you that if we understand the words in the right sense — not in the sense of our modern philistine language but in that of the ancient languages where living worlds were behind each word — then the Gospel of Saint Mark comes alive again and receives new force. With our modern language, however, it takes many circumlocutions to find again what was simply present in the words in ancient languages. When we say that human beings live on the earth and develop their I, and that they formerly lived on the moon where the angels went through the human stage, we are expressing what lies behind the words, "Behold, I send my angel before human beings." These words cannot be understood without prior knowledge of what spiritual science offers. People in our time should be honest and admit that the words at the beginning of Saint Mark's Gospel are incomprehensible. Instead, in petty pride they declare spiritual science a fantasy that reads all kinds of things into what they supposedly just know. However, they do not really know it.

Today the principle of rewriting sacred documents for each epoch, as was done in ancient Persia, is no longer practiced. Thus, the divine spiritual word, as presented in the Zend-Avesta, was transformed again and again. The Persian bible was rewritten seven times and what exists today is the last form. Anthroposophy has to teach people how necessary it is to rewrite the books containing the holy secrets in each epoch. For especially if we want to preserve the grand old style, we should not try to stay as close as possible to the ancient wording. That can't be done; the old words are no longer understood. Instead, we must try to translate the ancient wording into the immediate understanding of our time. That is what we have tried to do this summer with the Book of Genesis. You saw that many of the words had to be changed. Perhaps today you have got an idea of how the words must also be changed in the Gospel of Saint Mark.

LECTURE FOUR

The Universal Human:
The Unification of Humanity
through the Christ Impulse
BERN, JANUARY 9, 1916

BASICALLY, SPIRITUAL SCIENCE aims at understanding humanity in its essence, tasks, and strivings in the course of evolution. We have often talked about how the outside world misunderstands our spiritual science. This is largely because people nowadays have a hard time getting used to certain fundamental truths — truths that simply must be perceived and acknowledged if we are to understand the life and nature of humanity at all.

Let us begin today by asking what modern scientific thinking, whose great and significant triumphs over the last four centuries we must fully acknowledge and appreciate, is based on. It is based on what it can perceive, on what is manifest, in physical existence. Now, of course, it goes without saying that first we trust in what we perceive as so-called reality in our environment, and then we try to explain this reality on the basis of all that we find within its domain. It is naturally difficult for us to be aware at the outset that this reality itself may well contain an element of semblance or illusion, that it may well be deceiving us. Those who truly want to understand spiritual science must first overcome this stumbling block. They must realize that the reality around us can indeed deceive us — it can mislead us into interpreting it falsely. Much of what we have

69

learned in spiritual science over the years has convinced us that immediate reality, as it surrounds us, may indeed be deceptive.

Today we will start from a particular point that can only be reached through spiritual science. In spiritual science we must first understand things; then, when we have understood them, we can find them confirmed in reality. Some of the most important things in spiritual science must first be understood before they can be seen. It would be easy to show that this same method is frequently applied in the outer world, notably in the sciences, but we will not go into that today. It is not always possible to develop everything from the beginning.

Now one aspect of the outer appearance or physiognomy of reality that is most apt to deceive us about this reality is the differences, the diversities among human beings. When we look at the human beings inhabiting the earth, we realize that no two of them are alike on the physical plane. Here in the physical realm all human beings are different from one another. Once we have accepted this diversity of human beings as a fact — I mean the diversity of their physical bodies — it is quite natural that people then try to find out, on the basis of the facts of earthly life, why human beings are different, why they look so different.

However, from the point of view of spiritual science we see something very different. According to spiritual science, if we consider only the forms the physical body can take through the forces of the earth, we find that human beings could not be different but rather would all have to be alike and have the same outer form. Indeed, the forces that exist on earth to give us our physical shape are such that if only these formative forces were to work on us, we would all have the same outer, physical form. This is because the physical human body has undergone a long preparation. We know it was prepared through the epochs of Saturn, Sun, and Moon.[1] It was prepared by forces that worked during these three epochs in such a way that the forces of the earth itself could influence our physical body in no other way than to give it a uniform shape if they had indeed been the only forces at work. I might put it this way: Through all the forces that have been incorporated into our physical body during the Saturn, Sun, and Moon epochs, we human beings are so fortified against any diversities coming from earthly forces that if we were left to the earthly forces alone, we would be alike everywhere on earth. Spiritual science, therefore, must start from the fact that a single and uniform shape is predestined for humanity so far as the terrestrial forces are concerned.

Even if we consider just the difference between male and female what I have just said is true. This difference is not caused by the work of earthly forces; it is the result of quite other forces, which we will speak of presently. Thus, we can assume a certain totality of earth forces that works formatively upon human beings and wants to produce absolutely identical human forms everywhere on earth.

Of course, we must now ask why human beings are so different after all. We know we must consider not only our physical body, but also the etheric body that stands behind it. Spiritual science shows us that while we should all be alike in our physical body, in regard to our etheric body we must be different because earthly forces are not the only ones that work on our etheric body. Forces coming out of the cosmos work on our etheric body, forming and shaping it.

We must therefore distinguish between the uniform earthly forces working all over the earth that would make all human forms the same and the forces working out of the universe on the earth, making each etheric body different. We can see the differences between etheric bodies through spiritual scientific research. At the one extreme are those etheric bodies that have strong forces and are tough, retaining their form almost as much as we do our physical form. This is one kind of etheric body. There is a second kind that is mobile, like something that is fluttering and always in movement, flowing and moving. But these two kinds of etheric bodies still reveal themselves in such a way that we can describe their inner tone and shading as being more or less alike. There is another kind of etheric body that is inwardly tinted, inwardly shimmering, not uniform in color but having various tones and colors. There is a fourth kind of etheric body that has one primary color throughout its whole substance, but this color changes over time though we cannot pinpoint other than purely inward causes for this. These etheric bodies are not shimmering in different colors or shaded in many tones; they have only one color, but they change it in the course of time. We may call them chameleon-like etheric bodies.

Then there are those etheric bodies that have a strong tendency to light up inwardly, growing at times brighter and brighter. Other etheric bodies have a powerful faculty to reproduce the harmonies of the spheres. Finally, there are those etheric bodies that appear especially in inventive people and persons of genius — etheric bodies that, if I may say so, reveal forces within them that are rare and strange in this earthly world. Whereas the above-mentioned six kinds of etheric bodies are found among ordinary, even average, human beings, the last kind of etheric body produces the type of human being with powerfully developed faculties, those we often say are "not of this earth" — poets, artists, and the like.

It is not by arbitrarily picking the number seven that we distinguish these seven forms of etheric bodies. We simply have to count, and we find no others besides those I have just described as typical. For this simple reason, there are seven kinds of etheric bodies. There are seven different kinds of human etheric bodies, and in the etheric bodies we have forces that are not earthly, but come in from the cosmos.

Our etheric body forms and molds the physical body. If only earthly forces worked on us, we would all be alike in our physical body. However, the influence of the etheric body makes us different. The astral body brings about further differences, such as those between male and female bodies, through forces it develops between death and a new birth, during the time when we prepare ourselves for the gender that karma requires us to have in the next incarnation.

But for the moment, let us just look at the etheric body. If we take only earthly forces into account, we can say that our physical bodies would have to be alike. However, because our etheric bodies differ in their constitution, composition, and structure in the cosmos, there would have to be seven groups of human beings. This is the fact we gradually arrive at when we investigate the relationship between our etheric body and our physical body with the methods of spiritual science. Now this difference is connected with the racial diversities on the earth. Basically, because of this difference in etheric bodies, the several races can always be reduced to the number seven. Even though certain typical forms atrophy, and though natural science may distinguish fewer than seven basic races, there are really seven basic racial distinctions in the human species. These diversities are brought about by the etheric body; they do not result from the earthly forces that work during our evolution, but originate in cosmic forces.

Now, when we trace the evolution of the earth back into the Atlantean or even into the Lemurian epochs, we find that initially impulses and tendencies existed that would have prevented our physical body from developing the physiognomy it now has through the power of the etheric body — that is, the diversities. Instead, if everything had gone a certain way (we shall see directly in what way), the seven-colored etheric body would have brought about diversities in our physical form, but successively, one after the other. Thus, the etheric body would have created one form of human being in the fifth period of Atlantis, a second in the sixth period of Atlantis, a third in the seventh, a fourth in the first post-Atlantean period, a fifth in the second post-Atlantean period, a sixth in the third, and a seventh in the fourth post-Atlantean period, that is, in the Greco-Roman time.

That is what would have happened; various types of human beings would have appeared one after the other. Thus, in the fifth Atlantean period we would have had human beings in whose physical formation *one* type of etheric body would have predominated. In the sixth Atlantean period, the second of the etheric bodies just described would have been at work, and so on right until the fourth post-Atlantean period. That was the original conception. However, Lucifer and Ahriman opposed this; they did not want it to happen that way. They fought against this harmonious tendency of development in the evolution of humanity, and they managed to change the whole process so that various developments were shifted and displaced. While there should have been basically only one form of human being in the fifth Atlantean period that was to develop gradually into another type, Lucifer and Ahriman preserved the form of the fifth Atlantean period into the sixth, and again that of the sixth Atlantean period into the seventh, and even into the time after the Atlantean flood.

Thus, forms that should have disappeared remained. Instead of racial diversities developing consecutively, older racial forms remained unchanged and newer ones began to evolve at the same time. Instead of the intended consecutive development of races, there was a coexistence of races. That is how it came about that physically different races inhabited the earth and are still there in our time although evolution should really have proceeded as I have described it. Even when we consider only what resulted from the development of the etheric body, we see everywhere that Lucifer and Ahriman play their part in the earthly evolution of humanity.

Now we must ask what the intended consecutive development of humanity up until the Greco-Roman epoch meant in the larger cosmic context. As we know, around the Atlantean time, human souls gradually came down from the planets to which they had ascended. You may remember that I described in my *An Outline of Occult Science* that the souls had ascended and then came down again and that the life of earthly incarnations, properly speaking, begins with their descent.[2] Thus, the I of human beings, their individualities, would have gone through the various human forms

mentioned above in consecutive periods. In the fifth Atlantean period, the I would have had one human form, in the
sixth another, in the seventh again another; in the first
post-Atlantean epoch it would have had yet another form,
and so on. We would all have lived through these types of
humanity, one after the other.

Indeed, it was planned that human beings would thus
complete the necessary schooling of human individuality by
passing through various etheric formations that had different effects on their physical body. In fact, according to the
original plan, there could have been a type of human being
on the earth who would have been the result, as it were, of
seven successive periods of development, each of which
would have contributed to the perfection of that human
type. In the fifth post-Atlantean period, then, there would
have been one united type of human being spread over the
whole face of the earth.

However, Lucifer and Ahriman interfered and thwarted
the original design. As a result, the ancient Greeks could
only dream of an ideal, superhuman type, which they tried
to represent in various ways, for example, in the form of
Apollo, Zeus, or Athena. They could not fully encompass
this type simply because it did not really exist. But if we
have a sense for Greek sculpture, we can feel how the
ancient Greeks dreamed of a uniform, perfect, beautiful
type of human being that should have developed. This
development did not occur because Lucifer and Ahriman
preserved older racial forms that had developed, so that
there was a coexistence of races rather than a succession.

In the fourth post-Atlantean period, in the Greco-
Roman era, human evolution was faced with the fact that
what the gods guiding the evolution of the earth had

intended for the outer forms on this earth had not been realized because of the luciferic-ahrimanic influence. The spirits of the hierarchy of form had intended that the harmonious working of the various hierarchies of form should really lead to a human type with perfect physical development. As it turned out, the ancient Greeks could only dream of this perfect type and express it in their art.

It is a deeply moving experience to realize in the course of spiritual research why the Greeks created such perfection in their plastic art. They did it because through a soul-spiritual instrument they perceived that Lucifer and Ahriman had disappointed the good divine-spiritual beings, whose plans for humanity were different from the development that actually occurred. What should have developed through the work of these good divine-spiritual beings weighed on the ancient Greeks' minds, and so they wanted to at least represent it even though it did not exist in outer reality. It is great and wonderful and also deeply moving to behold these inner forces of human evolution that appear there in artistic forms, striving to express what could not be achieved in outer reality. Such insights shed new light on Greek art as it was developed so uniquely and unrepeatably at that time.

The Greek era was also the time when humanity faced a crisis because of the luciferic-ahrimanic influence. Lucifer and Ahriman had caused races to live side by side instead of one after the other. At the same time, however, all the forces the spirits of form were pouring into human evolution on the earth were immobilized. Now they could do no more than stimulate and inspire the creative imagination of the Greeks so that it developed as I have described it. The spirits of form had to decide whether the human race should continue to develop so that human beings would never again be united in earthly evolution. For this indeed is what would have happened. If earthly evolution had continued beyond the fourth, the Greco-Roman period, in the same way it was prior to that, then humanity would have become separated into seven groups due to luciferic and ahrimanic forces. These seven groups would have been as different from each other as the various species of animals. Animal species do not understand each other, but regard each other as foreign. Similarly, toward the end of the fourth post-Atlantean period and in the fifth one, in which we live, people would have had to develop more and more the view that there are seven groups of human beings on earth that see each other as completely different species. This view would still have prevailed in our time; in fact, the separation between the seven groups would not yet have reached its culmination or completion, but would still be developing and widening. The term "human being" for all people on earth would have seemed wrong; we would have had seven different terms, one for each of the seven groups.

Therefore, in the fourth post-Atlantean age, in the Greco-Roman period, something had to be done in the universe to forestall the development that threatened to result in the future, at the end of earth evolution, namely, the evolution of seven groups of human beings, each called by a different name, just as each animal species has a different name. These groups would not have regarded each other as belonging to the same species, and at most there would have been handed down to them some copy of the Greek forms, such as the statues of Zeus or Apollo. They would have regarded these statues as something alien to them — something that could never have existed on earth.

Precautions had to be taken to prevent such a development. Physical evolution had already gone too far and could not be changed anymore. Therefore, precautions had to be taken for our etheric body; an impulse had to enter our etheric body that would counteract the separating of earthly humanity into seven groups. This impulse that was to counteract the growing fragmentation of humanity and that was to make it possible for the term "human being" to retain — and, in fact, increase — its true meaning over the whole face of the earth was the Mystery of Golgotha, which we can now see in a new light.

The first attempt that had been made with earthly humanity before the luciferic and ahrimanic impulses interfered in evolution was to create unity among human beings everywhere through the forming of the physical body. This attempt by the spirits of form failed because of luciferic-ahrimanic interference. But it could not be allowed to fail altogether; precautions had to be taken to prevent complete failure and to immobilize and offset the work of Lucifer and Ahriman. The physical body could no longer be worked on as was originally intended; therefore, the etheric body had to be worked on. This was done by the divine-spiritual being we have so often spoken of — the Christ Being — taking on human form at the time in human evolution when the possibility to express the archetype of humanity was the greatest.

At what period in human evolution was this? All the forces that counteract the original, identical design of our physical body are at work in us mostly in the first seven years of life, when the physical body is still soft and pliant. They do not allow our physical body to become the same everywhere, but from within the body they immobilize the

forces for the original identical design.[3] These opposing
forces can still go on working in the second seven years
until puberty; indeed, they can even continue to work in
the third and fourth seven-year periods during the development of the astral body and the sentient soul. However, in
the middle of the development of the intellectual or mind
soul, which evolved above all in the fourth post-Atlantean
or Greco-Roman time, the extra-earthly forces are less and
less able to reach us. And in the very midst of this
development, that is, in the period between our twenty-
eighth and thirty-fifth years, they have least access to us. If
we add two years at the beginning of this period and
subtract two years at the end, the time in question is that
between the thirtieth and the thirty-third year. In the time
following those years, extra-earthly forces once more have
the greatest influence. The period from the thirtieth to the
thirty-third year, however, is the time of the greatest
influence of earthly forces on the human being. And if in
this period of three years there remained only the degree of
diversity that existed in younger years and only what is to
appear in later years would be added — in short, if only
what works on human beings between the thirtieth and the
thirty-third year remained effective, then people would
indeed be much more alike.

Christ had to use these three years — very special and
unique years — to unite with those earthly forces in human
beings that had retained most of the earthly element in the
human being. To this end, as we have discussed, the body
for Christ was prepared through the two Jesus bodies up to
the thirtieth year. Then, from the thirtieth to the thirty-
third year, Christ took possession of this body. Where the
earth forces were most active and where deformations could

have set in, there no further development was possible, and physical death occurred. Thus, the sun-being, Christ, really entered into the earth sphere and united with the whole etheric body of the earth, as I have often explained. He then entered into the earth aura and now continues to work there. This sun-being must work for us in such a way that we realize more and more that in Christ the divine spirit was sent to us who was to counterbalance and redeem from within the separation and diversification in humanity created by Lucifer and Ahriman's opposition to the original impulses.

In outer human nature, the good spiritual beings work together with Lucifer and Ahriman. But what human beings originally, at the beginning of earth evolution, were intended to have on the outside, namely, uniformity and the applicability of the term "human being" everywhere on earth, was now to be brought forth out of the innermost essence of the human being through the Christ-Spirit. It is one of the many meanings of the Mystery of Golgotha that with the Christ-Spirit something was given to the earth that, when rightly understood, makes the name "human being" again applicable to all earthly humanity. The real substance of Christianity, which has already been partially revealed through its teachings, will be explored by those who, in regard to Christ, seek in the spiritual world what Christ is continually revealing in accordance with his words: "I am with you always, to the close of the age." When what can be conveyed to human beings in the name of Christ from within thus gradually becomes known, then, as a result, what Lucifer and Ahriman did in earthly humanity can more and more be made up for and redeemed.

We may, of course, ask now if there is any meaning in

this detour. This is really a childish question, and it is often raised by people who think themselves cleverer than the cosmic wisdom — and indeed there are many who aspire to such superior cleverness. Such people say, "If there are mighty divine beings, could they not have eliminated the luciferic-ahrimanic influence at the beginning of earthly evolution in order to protect their work?" This may be human wisdom, but in St. Paul's sense it is "folly with God." It is nothing more than mere human wisdom.

In our lectures, we must look at things as we are now doing, and then what has developed through the opposition of Lucifer and Ahriman does not seem absolutely evil to us, but only relatively evil. For let us now consider the other side of the matter. Let us assume the original, divine cosmic plan for the earth had been fulfilled. Imagine that in the regular course of evolution the Greco-Roman era would have arrived, as I have pointed out, and that beautiful, harmonious type of human being the Greeks dreamed of would not only have been created by their sculptors, but would have lived among them and would gradually have spread over the whole earth. All other human forms would gradually have disappeared, and only what lives in the Apollo type, the Zeus type, the Diana type, and the Athena type would have spread over the earth. Since such beings would have recognized each other as belonging to the same species, they would have given themselves the name "human being." Then the term "human being" would indeed have been applicable, and at the same time there would have been a sense of the equality of all people.

In that case, a human race of Grecian beauty would have spread over the earth, and in our age we would already see humanity approaching more and more this beautiful

Grecian type, which would reach its perfection when the earth arrives at its goal in the seventh post-Atlantean epoch, after which it will pass over into other stages of existence. However, human beings would have advanced to this common humanity in unfreedom — that is what we must bear in mind. We would have been *compelled* to see all human beings everywhere as the same beings. It is only because such an identical form did not develop that all the other things could happen that allow us to see others as different, so that each sees the other as unlike himself and does not love his neighbor as himself. You will probably understand that if human beings had really become outwardly as alike as the original divine-spiritual forces had intended if Lucifer and Ahriman had not interfered, the feeling that one must love one's neighbor as oneself would necessarily have developed. There would not have been any choice; for anything else would have seemed to be nonsense, both in terms of feeling and of perception.

However, this development was not supposed to come from the outside because then it would have made us into beings who love automatically — that is, we would have loved others because they are our own kind, but without knowing the force that urges us to this love. Thus, what would otherwise have come to us in unfreedom was prepared for freedom through Lucifer and Ahriman's opposition. This sanction of the opposition is therefore inherent in the original plan of divine wisdom. Indeed, we may say that in still earlier periods of earthly evolution, the opposition against the harmonious progressive divine-spiritual powers was created precisely so that it could later bring about freedom.

At this point, we must realize that our concepts must

change when we leave the sphere of physical observation and ascend to a higher order of perception. Many of you probably know that philosophy speaks of antinomies, and that Kant has even gone so far as to claim that it can be proven with equal conclusiveness that the two statements "the world is infinite in terms of space" and "the world is finite in terms of space" are correct. Similarly, both "the world has had a beginning" and "the world has had no beginning" can be proven conclusively. Why is this? It is because logic does not apply when we come into a sphere that can no longer be comprehended by physical means. We finally have to realize that our physical logic works neither in the realm of philosophy nor anywhere else where we concern ourselves with other than physical forms of existence. We must not make the mistake of looking at the opposition of Lucifer and Ahriman as we would at the antagonism between a good and an evil person on earth. This kind of mistake occurs when we continue to carry over the earthly into the super-earthly realm.

Most people picture Ahriman and Lucifer as evil beings — albeit much more intensely evil than human beings. But this is not true; we must keep in mind that certain earthly feelings we associate with our concepts lose their meaning when we go beyond the earthly realm. Thus we cannot say that there are good gods on the one hand and the evil gods Ahriman and Lucifer on the other. We must not assume that a trial should be held in the universe where a highly qualified cosmic judge would sit on the cosmic judgment seat and sentence Lucifer and Ahriman to be locked up once and for all, so that only the good gods can get to work. True, locking somebody up can at times make sense in earthly life; in the cosmos it would not make any sense because there such ideas and concepts have no meaning. The opposing forces were created by the good gods themselves in an earlier period so that they would be able to bring to bear their full force for the development I have described.

For freedom to enter in so that human beings did not develop an unfree love through their outer shape or form, the luciferic and ahrimanic elements had to be part of our evolution. Only in this way can we arrive from within ourselves at the unity indicated by the term "humanity." Thus, the gods allowed humanity to be fragmented by the opposing forces, so that later, after their bodily nature had been thus separated, human beings could again be brought into a unity in their spiritual nature through Christ.

This is one of the meanings of the Mystery of Golgotha: the attainment of the unity of humanity from within. Externally human beings are becoming more and more different. The result will be not sameness but difference over the earth, and human beings must exert all the more force from within to attain unity. There will always be setbacks in this process of achieving unity — we can see them coming if we look for them. What was actually intended only for an earlier epoch is preserved into a later epoch, and what was to create differences in consecutive periods coexists. Human beings form different groups, and while they are struggling for unity all over the world in the name of Christ, through the Christ impulse, differences remain as aftereffects and setbacks. Such differences will always exist because human beings will only gradually be able to attain unity. At the same time, different groups will fight each other tooth and nail about everything concerning their outer life. There are setbacks from earlier epochs that run counter to the Christ impulse, rather than in harmony with it.

Indeed, here we see a very profound meaning of this Christ impulse. Based on true knowledge, we can say Christ is our savior who keeps humankind from being fragmented into groups. This is not yet fully understood by all people because the old still exists alongside the new. Today, people hardly understand the community of life in the Christ impulse, and this is connected with the fact that this understanding must proceed from our innermost being. We must realize that the Christ impulse has worked in the earth aura for the last two thousand years, but has not been understood. As we have often emphasized, this Christ impulse can only be fully understood through what spiritual science gives us. It is only when a growing number of people can more and more grasp, think, and feel what actually entered our earthly evolution in the fourth post-Atlantean period that understanding for that event will increase. To expect modern humanity to understand the Christ impulse is really asking too much. After all, just think how unwilling people are to acknowledge that this fourth post-Atlantean period of evolution, the Greco-Roman epoch, is of such paramount, such mighty significance in human evolution. Just think how unwilling people are to recognize any such post-Atlantean age at all with the Greco-Latin epoch as its pivotal point. To accept such truths, people need to take in the ideas of spiritual science. Without them one cannot understand these things at all — that is, one cannot understand the evolution of humanity if one has not taken in these concepts.

We have to understand the significance of the spirits of form, who had intended to develop a homogeneous human race in seven successive stages. This homogeneous human race was fragmented by Lucifer and Ahriman, but the force that wants to spread the one name "human being" over all the earth and unto the end of time — in spite of the outer differences between people — was revived from within by the Christ impulse. One of the chief tasks of the immediate future is to understand that Christ stands between Lucifer and Ahriman and to grasp his significance in relation to them. Therefore, we must always call Lucifer and Ahriman by their true names — we must call a spade a spade, so to speak — and look to the Christ impulse as the one combating them and saving the earth from this one-sided luciferic-ahrimanic impulse. This is what must be presented more and more often.

In our Dornach building we have therefore placed the statue *The Representative of Humanity* in the most prominent place; it presents the archetype of humanity that is to be recreated by Christ from within, surrounded by the luciferic-ahrimanic elements.[4] That is the meaning of this central statue in our building. Looking at this central figure, people will realize that this is indeed what the good gods had intended. The human race was fragmented, Lucifer and Ahriman made their appearance, but the Christ impulse triumphs and recreates from within, from within us, what was originally intended for the outside. In the process, our freedom is created. Our building and what will be in it are to place before humanity what must be accomplished in terms of understanding human evolution. What is most needed for humanity in the immediate future is to be revealed in our building; we want people to understand human evolution showing and telling them what is most important for the near future.

Of course, many objections can be raised, and some of them have already been brought to our attention. After seeing the paintings and sculptures in the Goetheanum, some people have said that a true work of art must be understandable immediately to everyone without requiring an explanation. Here, on the other hand, people need theoretical explanations to understand our art works. Well, if people would only think a little! Imagine a Turk, for example, understanding nothing at all except what is contained in the Koran, a Turk who has heard nothing about Christ except that he must fight against Christianity. Suppose you took this Turk to see the *Sistine Madonna* and showed it to him without any explanations. Naturally, a work of art can only be understood by those who live in the same spiritual stream out of which the work was created. Thus, our ideal figure surrounded by Lucifer and Ahriman will only be understood by those who live in our spiritual stream.

This is true for all works of art in all ages: they are comprehensible only to those who live in the same spiritual stream. Only within that stream are they true works of art. The spiritual orientation must be inherent in them. Those who understand Raphael's *Sistine Madonna* or, let us say, his *Transfiguration* must know something of the spiritual stream in which the pictures were created. Similarly, to understand what they have seen in our building, people must have some element belonging to our spiritual stream in their souls and hearts. If they have this element within them, then the work of art must speak for itself, and no labels, identifying names, or other comments will be needed to explain or interpret it.

For example, when people look at one of our glass

windows, they see in the bottom part a kind of coffin with a dead man in it; above that, they see an old man, a youth, a young woman, and a child standing on a winding path. If people have taken in our spiritual stream, they will realize that this is the review of life. Immediately after we have passed through the gate of death, we will see the course of our earthly life in reverse. Of course, you have to know this fact to make sense of the picture in the window. But if you know this, then the picture works by virtue of what it contains, just as the *Sistine Madonna* works upon those who know the Christian history behind it, but it has no such effect on the Turk. By the same token, what is presented in our building cannot work upon those who have not taken in our spiritual stream. These things just have to be seen in the right way.

Today, I wanted above all to explain that Christ was that spirit from the cosmos who, in the course of earthly evolution, brought spiritually what was originally intended for our outer form but could not develop externally, because we would then have become automatons of love and equality. On the physical plane there prevails the fundamental law that everything must operate through antitheses, through polarities. The gods could not simply have sent down Christ at the very beginning of earth evolution, as our naive wisdom might suggest they should have done. For then the antithesis of external fragmentation and inner concentration could never have developed. Humanity, however, must live in this antithesis and polarity. We have the right feelings for Christ only when we see in him the savior, rescuing humanity from dispersion and separateness; only then can Christ fill our own innermost I. Christianity lives wherever people are able to understand this union of all humanity through Christ. In the future, it will not matter much whether what Christ is will still be called by that name. However, a lot will depend on our finding in Christ the spiritual uniter of humanity and accepting that external diversity will increase more and more.

We will also have to accept that there will still be many setbacks for this spiritual understanding of the Christ impulse. What developed at the same time instead of consecutively will for a long time continue to evoke forces that fight against a spiritual understanding of global human equality. There will be many and terrible onslaughts, and, for the most part, their purpose will be to continue the luciferic-ahrimanic war against the Christ impulse. And it will be one of the greatest, most beautiful and significant achievements of our age if we can be among the few who understand this thought of the unifying of all human beings, who understand how remnants of the luciferic-ahrimanic elements strive to bring to the fore what is unique in various groups of human beings so as to exclude all others. It is very difficult to say anything at this time about the final outcome of these matters. As human hearts are now, to speak about that outcome would only be upsetting and bewildering; it may lead to opposition, perhaps even to hatred and abuse rather than to working in accordance with the Christ impulse. However, what can be said about this principle in the Christ impulse, namely, the salvation of humanity out of bodily fragmentation into spiritual unity, must be told, for it must become more and more effective in human evolution.

We have to be able to face calmly and courageously the increasing diversity in human nature because we know that we can carry a word into all these diversities that is not merely a word of speech but one of power. Though there may be groups that fight against each other and though we may even belong to one of them, we know that we can bring something that will express: "It is no longer I who live, but Christ who lives in me" into every group. We know that this "Christ who lives in me" will not lead to the forming of groups; rather, it will bring about the spreading of the glory of the name "human being" over the whole earth.

The understanding of spiritual science brings to life the realization that we can carry the power that comes from the words "It is no longer I who live, but Christ who lives in me" into the groups that are fighting each other — no matter into which group we bring our I. This is one of the practical and moral-ethical aspects of our strivings in spiritual science. With the force of these words we bring something into the group that does not belong exclusively to one or the other group but to all humanity. It is only through this that we can arrive at a true spiritual understanding of Christianity.

It is the hallmark of mighty spiritual paths that they are finally expressed in simple words. Think of the simple words that can express the whole of Christianity, which has permeated the world for nearly two thousand years. But these simple words can only be found on the basis of big, long-term developments. These simple words that express Christianity were not just there all at once; they had to be worked for. We must be aware that we are among those people working to make it possible that someday simple words may be found to express, in a basic, elementary way, the truths we have to spread and develop today. Without such development the simple could never come about. We may not yet be able to put our spiritual science into simple words in any language — words that would condense it on a quarter of a page — so that all striving people would understand it, as was done for Christianity when it originated two thousand years ago. Yet, we can be sure that those simple words will contain something of what I said today, something that will direct our attention to the Greco-Roman age, especially to the Mystery of Golgotha during that time, as well as to the contrast or polarity between Christ and Lucifer-Ahriman.

What can be seen everywhere will be concentrated in a few simple words that can then be handed down to future humanity in the same way as the commandment, "You shall love the Lord your God with all your heart, and with all your soul, and with all your strength, and with all your mind; and your neighbor as yourself." Just as this commandment expresses something that had to be attained as a result of a long development, so, in the future, the findings of spiritual science will be put into simple words, and then all people will understand them.

This requires our spiritual work, for the simple can only arise in the spiritual evolution of humanity when people have been willing to spend long periods of time learning about the details. You are called upon to help in this development, which will lead to something appearing to people in bright clarity, something we cannot yet express because we do not have the words for it in our languages, yet something spiritual science works toward. When you feel you belong to such a spiritual stream, and feel at home in it, because you see that it is necessary for human evolution, then you have the right understanding of our spiritual movement — you belong to it in such a way that you rightly understand the greatest of its goals based on your increasing understanding of the contrast between Christ and Lucifer-Ahriman. You understand that this contrast is vital and had to exist.

This is what I wanted to bring before your souls today. It is all connected with the question of the meaning of our whole earthly evolution. For when spirits from other planets look down upon the earth and ask what the meaning of this earthly evolution is, they will understand it when they learn about the Mystery of Golgotha. Everything that happens in the course of earthly evolution has its meaning only through the Mystery of Golgotha. The Mystery of Golgotha radiates out into the cosmos and imparts to everything else that radiates out from the earth its meaning, its central meaning.

Notes

LECTURE ONE

[1] Johann Gottlieb Fichte, 1762–1814, German philosopher. The statement Steiner refers to here can be found in Fichte's *Grundlage der gesamten Wissenschaft* ("Foundation of Science"), 1794, note to Paragraph 4.

[2] Rudolf Steiner, *The East in the Light of the West*, vol. 113 in the Collected Works, and Edouard Schuré, *Children of Lucifer*, both in one volume, (Blauvelt, NY: Spiritual Science Library, 1986).

[3] The so-called Egyptian Gospel is an apocryphal gospel of which only fragments have survived.

LECTURE THREE

[1] See Rudolf Steiner, *The Gospel of St. John*, vol. 103 in the Collected Works, repr. (Hudson, NY: Anthroposophic Press, 1988), *The Gospel of St. John and Its Relation to the Other Gospels*, vol. 112 in the Collected Works (Spring Valley, NY: Anthroposophic Press, 1982), *The Gospel of St. Luke*, vol. 114 in the Collected Works, repr. (London: Rudolf Steiner Press, 1988), and *The Gospel of St. Matthew*, vol. 123 in the Collected Works, repr. (London: Rudolf Steiner Press, 1985).

[2] Rudolf Steiner, *Portal of Initiation: A Rosicrucian Mystery Drama* (Blauvelt, NY: Steinerbooks, 1981).

LECTURE FOUR

[1] These names do not refer to present-day planets but to ancient evolutionary stages and are therefore capitalized.

[2] Rudolf Steiner, *An Outline of Occult Science*, vol. 13 in the Collected Works, repr. (Spring Valley, NY: Anthroposophic Press, 1989).

[3] Editor's note: The transcript seems to be faulty here. The original reads: "They [the opposing forces] let it [the physical body] become the same; they make it identical from within." This obviously contradicts not only the statements directly preceding this passage, but also the lecture as a whole.

[4] The statue is Rudolf Steiner's wood sculpture *The Representative of Humanity*. It survived the burning of the first Goetheanum and stands now in the second Goetheanum.

www.ingramcontent.com/pod-product-compliance
Lightning Source LLC
LaVergne TN
LVHW091204080426
835509LV00006B/829